T0362922

PUBLISHED BY BOOM BOOKS
boombooks.biz

ABOUT THIS SERIES

....But after that, I realised that I knew very little about these parents of mine. They had been born about the start of the Twentieth Century, and they died in 1970 and 1980. For their last 50 years, I was old enough to speak with a bit of sense.

I could have talked to them a lot about their lives. I could have found out about the times they lived in. But I did not. I know almost nothing about them really. Their courtship? Working in the pits? The Lock-out in the Depression? Losing their second child? Being dusted as a miner? The shootings at Rothbury? My uncles killed in the War? Love on the dole? There were hundreds, thousands of questions that I would now like to ask them. But, alas, I can't. It's too late.

Thus, prompted by my guilt, I resolved to write these books. They describe happenings that affected people, real people. The whole series is, to coin a modern phrase, designed to push your buttons, to make you remember and wonder at things forgotten. The books might just let nostalgia see the light of day, so that oldies and youngies will talk about the past and re-discover a heritage otherwise forgotten. Hopefully, they will spark discussions between generations, and foster the asking and answering of questions that should not remain unanswered.

BORN 1944?
WHAT ELSE HAPPENED?

RON WILLIAMS

AUSTRALIAN SOCIAL HISTORY

BOOK SIX IN A SERIES OF 35 FROM
1939 to 1973

War Babies Years	1939 to 1945	7 Titles
Baby Boom Years	1946 to 1960	15 Titles
Post Boom Years	1961 to 1969	13 Titles

BOOM, BOOM BABY, BOOM

BORN IN 1944? WHAT ELSE HAPPENED?

Published by Boom Books, Wickham, NSW, Australia

web: boombooks.biz

Email: jen@boombooks.biz

Creator: Williams, Ron, 1934- author

Title: Born in 1944? What else happened?

ISBN: 9781502486608 (paperback)

Australia--History--Miscellanea--20th century.

Cover images: National Archives of Australia .

A5954, 661/12 Prime Minister John Curtin;

A11663, PA189 Nurses travelling on troop ship to Europe, 16 November;

A11663, PA189 Large contingent of AIF sailing from Melbourne;

 J2364, 677/9 Mechanics in training.

TABLE OF CONTENTS

BACKGROUND DATA

King of England	George VI
Prime Minister of Australia	John Curtin
Leader of Opposition	Robert Menzies
Governor General	Lord Gowrie
British PM	Winston Churchill
American President	Theodore Roosevelt
Pope	Pius XII

THE ASHES

1936 - 7	Australia 3 - 0
1938	Drawn 1 - 1
1946 - 7	Australia 2 - 0

THE MELBOURNE CUP

1943	Dark Felt
1944	Sirius
1945	Rain Bird

ACADEMY AWARDS

BEST ACTOR	Paul Lukas
BEST ACTRESS	Jennifer Jones

INTRODUCTION TO THE SERIES

I was five years old when the War started. But even at that early age, I was aware of the dread, and yet excitement, that such an epoch-making event brought to my small coal-mining town. At the start, it was not at all certain that it would affect us at all, but quickly it became obvious that everybody in the nation would become seriously involved in it.

The most immediate response I remember was that all the Mums (who still remembered WWI) were worried that their sons and husbands would be taken away and killed. After that, I can remember radio speeches given by Chamberlain, Churchill, Lyons, Menzies, and Curtin telling of hard times ahead, but promising certain victory over our wicked foes.

For a young boy, as the War years went on, reality and fantasy went hand in hand. As I heard of our victories, I day-dreamed of being at the head of our Military forces, throwing grenades and leading bayonet charges. I sank dozens of battleships from my submarine that was always under attack. And I lost count of the squadrons of Messerschmitts that I sent spiraling from the sky. Needless to say, I was awarded a lot of medals and, as I got a bit older, earned the plaudits of quite a few pretty girls.

But, mixed in with all this romance, were some more analytical thoughts. Every day, once the battles got going, I would go to the newspapers' **maps** of where the battlelines currently were. One for the Western front, one in North Africa, and a third in Russia. Later, another in the Pacific. Then I would examine them minutely to see just how far we had moved, backwards or forward. I read all the reports, true and false, and gloated when it was said we were winning, and shrank away at our losses.

At the personal level, I remember the excitement of getting up at 4am on a few days when nearby Newcastle was under submarine attack. We went to our underground air-raid shelter that we shared with a neighbour, and listened, and occasionally looked out, for some who-knows-what enemies to appear. It really was a bit scary.

I can remember too the brown-outs, and the black-outs, the searchlights, the tank-traps, the clackers that were given to wardens to warn of gas attacks, and the gasmasks that 20 town-wardens (only) carried, presumably to save a town of 2,000 people when needed. Then there was the rationing, the shortages of everything, and even the very short shirt tails that a perceptive Government decreed were necessary to win the War.

At the start of researching this book, everything started to come back to me. Things such as those above, and locations like Dunkirk, Tobruk, El Alamain, Stalingrad, and Normandy. Really, at this stage these names kept popping up, but I was at loss as to how significant they were. Also, names of people. Hitler and Mussolini I knew were baddies. But **how** bad? Chamberlain was always criticised for his appeasement, but what were his alternatives? Who **were** Ribbentrop and Molotov, and Tojo and Blamey, and what was Vichy France?

And finally, when war did come, and grind on, year after year, what effect did it have back here in Australia. How did we as a society cope with a world that just had to continue on, given that the sons and dads of the nation were actually being killed daily overseas? When the postman did his normal delivery and brought a letter saying your loved one is dead? What did we do when old jobs suddenly disappeared, and new ones were created a thousand miles away? When goods, long readily available, were no longer for sale? When everything changed?

It was all a hotch-potch to me when I started this series. At the end of it, I can say it is a lot clearer. I have sorted out the countable things like battles, locations, people, and rules and regulations. I can also appreciate the effects on society, though these can only be ascertained from what I **have** researched, and make no allowance for all that I might have missed.

In presenting this book, I have started every chapter with a look at the military events in the world, first the Pacific, then Europe and the Middle East. Then I come back to Oz to see how we are faring in a military sense within the nation. After that, I blunder about reporting and speculating on which aspects of life here were affected by these, and other ongoing matters.

So, despite all the talk about the War above, and despite the fact that **it** was the controlling influence on all of our lives, the **thrust of these books is about the social changes and** reactions that took place in this period, here in Oz.

AUSTRALIA'S LEGACY FROM 1943

By now, at the beginning of 1944, Australia was confident that she would **not** be invaded by the Japanese. It had been a near thing. **In the first half of 1942**, invasion seemed pretty likely. The Japs had conquered all of the south-west

Pacific, including Malaya, Singapore, and our nearest neighbor, Indonesia.

She had occupied the northern shores of New Guinea, and was trying to use the Kokoda Trail to come down to Port Moresby, just across the narrow sea to Australia. She had shelled Sydney and Newcastle from mini subs, bombed Darwin and other northern Oz cities, and sunk a couple of dozen ships off our coast. Many people thought Australia might actually be invaded, and a million more vowed we would fight to the death if we were.

During the second half of 1942, the menace slowly decreased. Australia was moving to what was called a "war economy" and the American forces were coming at a reasonable pace. So the Japs were held at bay, and gradually were forced back. For example, Oz teen-age lads drove them back off the Kokoda Trail, and then started to hound them along the northern shores of New Guinea.

The war economy meant that most able-bodied men were **somehow** called to duty to serve the needs of the nation. The Army was the obvious first place to put these conscripts and volunteers, and after that there were **various forms of recruitment** that took many men to far distant places. For example, they built long roads through Australia's north, they built hundreds of airfields, again mainly in the north, they worked to renovate harbours, or they built air raid shelters and ditches.

They were part of the **CCC, the Civil Construction Corps**, and were counted in the hundreds of thousands. Part of the apparatus of getting men, and women, **to serve in any capacity** was the much-despised **Manpower** organisation that **had a bad reputation for inefficiency, and inconsistency and for abusing its powers**.

Many of the CCC recruits worked in factories producing munitions and guns and even planes. In these factories, a fair number of women were also employed, at 90 percent of the male wages. This lower rate was because they were not called on to do heavy or dirty or dangerous jobs. In any case, everyone worked long hours, for six or more days per week, and at the end of 1942, **no annual leave was permitted to employees right across the nation.**

Women also made a large contribution through fund raising, providing home accommodation to servicemen on leave, knitting sox, and making camouflage nets. The number of ways that both men and women contributed to the nation's production was endless.

The fun of austerity. Our Government decided that if our military forces (including Americans) were to be properly equipped and fed, then our civilians had to consume less. So tea, butter, petrol, and clothing and materials were officially rationed, by issuing coupons.

As well as that, it restricted the manufacture of all sorts of goods, and made it virtually impossible for ordinary people to get them. Items such as car and bicycle tyres, toys, radio sets, tools, furniture, lollies and chocolates were difficult to get. It was illegal, subject to fines or imprisonment, to sell cakes with **pink** icing. Shirt tails were cut down to official lengths so that, if you moved, the shirt would come out of your pants. In brief, great austerity was imposed on the entire population. Thank heavens that a good black market was slowly developing.

At the start of 1943, the fear of invasion had gone, except among determined pessimists. So gradually, across the year, people got a little more restless under the Government regulations. They were less inclined to continue working under rotten or unsafe conditions, so strikes in some militant Unions grew more common. A few regulations were relaxed by Government.

For example, cars could show their lights at night, and no longer needed their lights hooded. The cladding over windows at night was no longer imperative. These were welcome signs for the future. Yet, **at the end of 1943, meat rationing was introduced**, so that we could send meat to our British friends. **At the start of 1944**, austerity was still very much the order of the day.

People were bearing up quite well. They **were** tired, genuinely tired. Most workers outside the home had been doing long shifts, and too many shifts, for two years. This brought in a lot of money, and **they were collectively better off than they had ever been before**. But they were sick of the War, and sick of all the talk about it. They just wanted it to be all over, and things to go back to normal. Yet they realised that there was still a long way to go before the Japs were defeated, and were resolved to go the full distance.

Probably the greatest worry at the time was the **war deaths and injuries**. Every day, in the newspapers, a list of the casualties was published. Sometimes 30 dead, sometimes 200 men dead, or 200 missing in action, or maimed. **The list was there every day**. For those who had men-folk in the war zones, their lives were filled with constant fear. They could get a dreaded message from the Army at any time, saying that a terrible fate had befallen their sons. So all day they looked out their windows, hoping the postman or telegram boy would go past their house. Sadly, thousands and thousands of times, they stopped right there.

CENSORSHIP AND PROPAGANDA

The strong arm of the Government surrounded the nation. Government censorship was designed to keep important information from the enemy, and to raise the morale of the population.

These officials pried into correspondence between soldiers and their family, listened to people talking in trams and trains, studied every word published in newspapers, and heard every word uttered by radio stations. They were looking for any leaks of important information.

This was, in theory, a valuable service that these bureaucratic officials were performing. However, as the nation witnessed time and time again during the war, **the officials employed went to great excess**.

For example, in 1943, the Press was allowed to publish the news of the sinking of an Oz ship off the coast of Western Australia. Two dozen people were killed, and the nation mourned their unfortunate deaths. But then it was revealed that **the incident had occurred one year previously** and had not been reported at the time.

There was general outrage that the Government thought that the nation could not be trusted to digest this information and keep its morale high. After all, in Britain, the authorities were announcing up-to-date info about the dozens of ships sunk every day. What was the difference with Australia, it was asked.

There was another set of bureaucracies that got the public offside. These related to anti-enemy propaganda. The most irritating thing about these was they treated citizens as if they were idiots. Every time we engaged the enemy on land, sea, or air – and we did this a dozen times a day – we got Press reports like "we attacked such-and-such and shot down 44 planes, and lost only three." The reports were so obviously wrong that, by the start of 1944, people were getting more reliable info from their **short-wave radios**. Enemy radio, hosted by British traitor Lord Haw Haw, or the Japanese Tokyo Rose, provided news that was exaggerated and subversive, but was based on facts, and usually up to date. At the start of the year, the news on local rumour-mills was often more reliable than much of the official news. Again, we will see more of this later.

WHAT WAS HAPPENING IN EUROPE?

In Europe, the war was being fought on a number of fronts. The big bangs were along the western edge of Russia, where the Nazi forces were facing slow extermination. Winter was now at hand, and along the whole battle-line, from the Baltic Sea in the north, down to the Ukraine on the Black Sea in the south, the Germans were being relentlessly routed. **Hitler must have been sorely regretting his unnecessary invasion of Russia two years earlier.**

For the Brits, on the so-called western front, **all fear of invasion had long since gone**, and interest was focusing on how and when some sort of invasion of the Continent could be done. All of Africa was now virtually back under

Allied control. Italy was now "half-liberated", and pro-Allies guerilla movements and saboteurs were active in all the nations that the Nazis had earlier conquered.

On top of that, the Brits with their American colleagues were, night after night, bombing all the major sites in Germany with tremendous bomb-loads. Most of the major cities of Germany, and of the conquered nations, received their fair share of bombs, and so too did railways, bridges, factories, and military installations.

As well as that, the Battle of the Atlantic at last showed signs of victory for the Allies. Up till now, Britain had held superiority with its surface navy, but **German submarines had been exacting a fearful toll**. Now, there were a few signs that Britain and America between them were destroying more enemy subs than could be built, and that the bombings of sub factories and bases were at last having their desired effect.

The major worry for the Brits, as for Australians, was that their menfolk were spread round Europe and as far as India and Burma, and even Singapore. Every person had a family member, or a neighbour, or a friend, who was in some sort of danger every day, and every person dreaded getting a terrible message from the military authorities.

Then there was the rationing, and the shortages, and still the occasional air-raid, the black-outs, the all-pervasive power of Government and their many dubious regulations. Britain was still a bleak place to live, yet it was filled with a cautious hope that there was a better world, maybe, just round the corner. Remember, if you can, the songs from the nation's sweetheart at the time, Vera Lynn. *"There'll be*

Blue Birds over the White Cliffs of Dover", and its haunting line "*and Billy will go to sleep, in his own little room once more.*" Then there was the promise that "*We'll Meet Again, don't know where, don't know when, but I know we'll meet again, some sunny day.*"

BACK IN OZ AGAIN

This nation was fully employed, most people were working overtime, so pockets were full of ready cash. The trouble, for some, was how to spend it. Many goods were rationed, and most others were in short supply. If you wanted to buy a car, you needed a good military-based reason, and all sorts of permissions. Clothing was rationed, and in any case, the fabrics were throw-backs, and there was no hint of fashion. Houses were not being built or bought, household fittings were not procurable, new bike tyres had disappeared, and buying cakes with **pink** icing could land you in goal. Everything was in short supply, even waste paper and cardboard.

Our frustrated spenders were constantly being told to put the money into a Series of Commonwealth War Loans, that opened every four months or so. The money from these loans was used to finance the war, and you won't be surprised to know that this was a very costly business.

Strikes were **officially** illegal, though the Labour Government, led by John Curtin, had a majority of only two in the Senate. This meant that the Trade Unions could call its bluff over strikes whenever they thought fit, and Curtin, scared of losing Union support, could only threaten and cajole. So, the bigger, more vocal unions, got away with dozens of strikes each month, without serious sanctions.

John Curtin was a beleaguered Prime Minister, with only that small majority.

Just as bad was the fact that he was saddled with a few Cabinet Ministers who could most charitably be described as "wild–cannons", who wanted to run their own war and society. Again, these men were dear to the Unions, so there was no chance that he could sack them. Still, he persevered, and worked most earnestly, with the result that he had become one of those very rare politicians who had the respect of almost everyone.

OVERSEAS VISITORS IN OZ

Japanese in Australia, 1944. In the early years of the War, aliens from different nations were generally harassed by the authorities, and the men were very often interned. This happened early on to those immigrant Italians and Germans **who had not been naturalised**, and they were taken away to places like farms to work out the war there. In earlier *books in this Series*, I described the heartaches that this brought.

When the **Italians** were arrested and taken away from their family, in Gestapo style in the earliest light of day, there was quite a public outpouring of sympathy for them. After all, these were the greengrocers, milk-bar owners, and small shop-keepers in many small towns and suburbs. No one could believe they would support Mussolini.

One group that escaped the publicity at the time was a small number of Japanese nationals who happened to be in Australia when Japan threw down its gauntlet. These were mainly people who were in Oz, for example, on business, and for whom there was no way out. These unlucky people were also interned, and worked at the pleasure of the Commonwealth for the duration.

With the Japs, there was no public hub-hub at all, and in fact their very existence was not revealed until after the War. Just as well perhaps, given the animosity that Australians felt to the Japanese at the time.

Another, **entirely different group of Japanese,** were the prisoners-of-war who had been captured in New Guinea. These men were shipped to Australia, and many of them ended up in a prison camp at Cowra in NSW. These were much more belligerent than the above internees, and **caused quite a stir later in the year**.

AMERICANS IN AUSTRALIA

There were plenty of **Yanks in Oz.** US soldiers and airmen had started coming rather early in 1942, and had come in increasing numbers ever since. Many of them were based near the major cities in Queensland, or in the Northern Territory. They fought in the later stages in New Guinea, and then were often shipped off to do battle in the Pacific islands. Their airmen were flying sorties all the time, bombing Japanese bases and harassing shipping.

Aussies had mixed feeling about these visitors. There was no doubt that their presence and supplies were turning the tide against the Japs. No one could gainsay this wonderful fact. On the other hand, everyone knew that their **purpose** here was not to defend Australia, but rather **to further American interests**. It just happened that **their aim** and **our aim** coincided, so we got the benefit of their presence.

Other, smaller, things grated on Aussies. MacArthur, their leader, had done a deal with Curtin that provided for food for US troops to be at a certain standard. But that standard was well above the level that Oz troops got, so the Americans were fed much better than the Australian troops. They had better uniforms in public, and so had an advantage with the girls when on leave. They bragged a lot, and droned on about what a great country America was, and how **great they were in battle, and** how **they** had already saved Australia. In all the city pubs round Australia, they were involved in brawls every Saturday night with Oz soldiers.

But these were small irritations in the scheme of things. Overall, the Yanks were welcome, and only a complete fool would say that they were not achieving a good result.

A BOATING TRAGEDY AVERTED

End of 1943. Early in the war, the Feds decreed that **no petrol** would be available to owners of **launches and small craft**. This meant that the craft were anchored in one spot, and **their engines could not be turned over,** nor could they be driven even the smallest distance. **Now**, it is reported that **small boat-owners** in NSW were **forming an Association** to make collective attempts to secure petrol to prevent their **boat engines from being ruined.**

January 15th. The Federal Government has decided **to issue** one to four gallons of **petrol** per month to owners of launches and small vessels.

MY RULES IN WRITING

I give you a few Rules I follow as I write. They will help you understand where I am coming from.

Note. Throughout this book, I rely a lot on reproducing Letters from the newspapers. Whenever I do this, I put the text in a different font, and indent it a little, and make the font somewhat smaller. **I do not edit the text at all.** The same is true for the News Items at the start of each Chapter. That is, I do not correct spelling or if the text gets at all garbled, I do not correct it. **It's just as it was seen in the Papers.**

Second Note. The material for this book, when it comes from newspapers, is reported as it was seen at the time. If the benefit of hindsight over the years changes things, then I might record that in my Comments. The info reported **thus reflects matters as they were seen in 1944.**

Third Note. Let me also apologise in advance to anyone I might offend. In a work such as this, **it is certain some people will think I got some things wrong**. I am sure that I did, but please remember, all of **this is only my opinion**. And really, my opinion does not matter one little bit in the scheme of things. **I hope you will say "silly old bugger", and shrug your shoulders, and read on.**

So now we are ready to plunge into 1944. Let's go, and I trust you will have a pleasant trip.

JANUARY: NEWS ITEMS

The Japanese were now depending on **fantastic lies** in their war propaganda **to explain away recent crushing defeats**, General Sir Thomas Blamey said. He added that it was only a matter of time and materials before Japan was beaten....

He pointed out that the plan **to release 20,000 men from the armed forces, for work on farms**, was being executed now, and would be complete in a few months.

Army figures for the year 1943 indicate that **635 Australian prisoners-of-war (in Asia) were released from captivity during the year**, and returned to Australia. Our current biggest group of POWs was **the 15,000 captured in Singapore**.

Leading manufacturers consider that there is no possibility of easing **the scarcity of ice chests for domestic use** this summer.

The NSW Chief Secretary has urged the Commonwealth to consider releasing **three trawlers from sequestration to increase the fish supply.** Many trawlers were grounded eighteen months ago so the **men could be released for Services.**

The Government said that cooks and other **workers employed in cafes and restaurants** will **not** be called up by Manpower for **work in hospitals**. This will frustrate Manpower, which was ready to put the plan into place.

From January 17th, **meat rationing by coupons** will become necessary. For a person over nine years of age, the ration will be from **two to four pounds per week**, depending on how much bone is included in the cut. Children under nine will receive a half ration.

8,000 sorties were sent out **last week** by the Allies in Europe. The numbers who returned were not released.

Coal mining was regarded as an essential industry. That meant that it was a so-called **protected industry**, so that its workers **were not called up for military or civilian service....**

The Coal Industry Tribunal announced that **mineworkers**, who refused to submit to Union discipline, had "**been released from the coal industry**". Their future would be decided by Manpower. This meant **military or civil service**, almost certainly away from home.

Several persons **were fined** in the Special Court yesterday for having been in possession of the **forged petrol ration coupons.**

News item. The Government has **withdrawn** the issue of **1,500,000 copies of a booklet** prepared for the start of **meat rationing.** Officials and Ministers would not comment on the reasons, but it is thought that some matters may have changed since the book was prepared. No estimates were available of the cost of the exercise.

The New Zealand Minister for mines said **the Government there had taken over 60 per cent of**

mines in the nation. This was because industrial unrest was too high, and it was thought that Government control could reduce it.

The drug hynacine, which is used in childbirth to produce **"twilight sleeps"** in childbirth, **has prevented seasickness** in 73 per cent of soldiers who participated in experiments.

The 1943 Archibald Prize was won by **Williams Dobell** for a **portrait** of Joshua Smith. Some people were astonished. They claimed that it was not a portrait, but a caricature.

Berlin was being pasted by bombs, and other German cities were copping it as well. Typically, about 2,000 pounds of bombs would be dropped each day, and **about 40 of our planes would not return. A terrible toll on both sides.**

Ten thousand people, 34 per cent of them women, are employed in the production of **Bristol Beaufort torpedo bombers in Australia.**

Fines totaling 300 Pounds were imposed on two defendants in Melbourne for breaches to the transport regulations. These involved **driving horses in vans long distances for the purpose of racing them.** For example, from Melbourne to Adelaide.

The Russian Commission investigating German brutality said that the bodies of about **15,000 Polish solders** had been **dumped in a mass grave at Katyn.**

MEAT RATIONING

Rationing of meat was introduced on January 15th for the civilian population. It was a tricky business working out the rules of how it would operate, and this led to much heartache. **For example,** suppose you wanted half a Pound of steak. A problem arose because **a single coupon allowed for a full pound**. Initially it was decided that the butcher should issue some sort of voucher saying that the customer still had a credit of half a pound, and that could be taken up later. But the question arose as to whether **other** butchers would recognize these credits.

In any case, the idea of issuing such credits was a nightmare for butchers and so this part of the scheme was made voluntary. The revised rule was that one coupon covered one pound of steak or part thereof. There were many cries of outrage, especially from **pensioners, (few of them with refrigerators or ice-boxes)**, who said that they only wanted **half** a pound, and so their meat ration was being effectively reduced.

There were thousands of issues like this. When a soldier came home on leave, what meat was he allowed? How could he get his coupons in a timely manner? Aliens sometimes ate parts of carcasses that Aussies would not eat. Were these meats be in category one, or two, or three or four? So how many coupons were to be taken by the frustrated butcher?

Correspondence on the matter was voluminous and was matched only by the number of grizzles in the community. I will present a few Letters on this matter in a minute.

First, though, I should point out that the rationing was caused by **a shortage of meat in Britain**. Australia had adequate supplies to feed this nation, and the hundred thousand American troops that we were responsible for. It .ẘås **the Brits** who were really suffering, and so we came to their rescue. We did this as a nation without question. **No one grizzled about rationing because our meat was going to the Brits. It was just part of our duty** and inclination to give any support we could to the Mother Country. What people often grizzled about was the administration and the bungled introduction of the scheme. Though, having said that, there was quite a variety of complaints and suggestions to choose from.

Letters, Already Harassed. From a busy mother's point of view, it will now be impossible to send children to the butcher before school because the whole thing is so complicated. It will cause many such as myself to walk two miles a day for a small allowance of meat.

Further, why are not all coupons perforated so that they can be easily torn out by shopkeepers? Would not a separate thin card of coupons be more useful for the meat ration, so that the butcher can handle the coupons himself and thus save the all-purpose ration book from grease and stains?

Letters, ONE FROM THE BUSH. Apparently "G" coupons must be cut from the book **in the butcher's presence**. I live out in the bush, and do not go into Gosford for weeks and sometimes months. The bus driver carries the mail, and also takes people's orders into Gosford and also brings them out at night. The bus probably carries 50 or 60 meat orders.

Are we expected to send our books in with our orders, or will we be allowed just to send the coupons in, the same as for tea and butter?

Letters, G Johnson. It is a pity that, in the interests on national health efficiency, a campaign could not be started to educate people to a proper appreciation of food values and treatment, and debunk **a lot of nonsense**, such as that gargantuan quantities of meat are necessary to vitality and strength, when they are, in fact, mainly a load on the digestion. It has been known for some years that our white breads and so-called wholemeal contain no food value or vitamins at all. Yet millers are permitted to go on producing this glutinous rubbish on which it has been proved that not even rats can obtain sufficient nourishment to live healthily; while the best and most vital part of our superb wheat is destroyed.

It would certainly be a worth-while investment if children from their middle years at school were given a thorough course in dietetics, as it is upon this matter that their health, happiness, and prosperity depend to a greater extent than anything else.

News Item. Mr Walter Howlett, the only butcher in the village of Currabubula, intends to close his shop forever on Saturday because he is "not a good enough scholar to handle the coupon system."

"Customers would get angry with me for being so slow," he said. "Apart from the coupons, the whole scheme would be beyond me." Mr Howlett, who is 75, has been supplying Currabubula residents with meat for 45 years.

"My customers are in a bad way," he said, "because the nearest place where they can obtain meat is Werris Creek, nine miles away. I am sorry to leave the business I have built up over the years, but there is no alternative. It's just too complicated for me."

Letters, Paul Royle. All true lovers of animals must be upset at **the destruction of dogs** at the Dogs' Home at the request of **people who fear meat rationing**. The hysterical owners who have already sacrificed their pets are not true lovers of animals, or, if so, are very ignorant. Nearly every paper has published formulae for animal (substitute) food, and any veterinary surgeon can give guidance to anyone who really wishes to save their helpless dumb friends.

Letters, Pal O' Mine. People are sacrificing faithful pets, in the majority of cases, unnecessarily. Surely meat rationing need not make it impossible for the keeping of at least one pet in the home, if one really cares sufficiently to give the matter a little thought.

Letters, Australian Mother. Would it not be a fine gesture if one at least of the many women's organisations were to hold out a helping hand to the Government, and educate women-folk on how to manage and make up nourishing dishes with the amount of meat available? It is not always quantity that counts.

If the housewives of Britain and other countries have had to manage, surely those of Australia are not going to squeal. Many will find they are better in health, as the average Australian eats too much meat. During the suffragette movement years ago, those who went on hunger strikes while in prison found that, owing to eating less, their health was much improved, and many later turned their attention to dieting.

Letters, Mrs E Stead. It mainly rests with the housewife to make meat rationing a success. If the week's menu is planned ahead with an alternative list in case of inability to buy the required items, this will not only save the butcher's time but our own. Let us housewives set an example to the rest of Australia and show how we can make sacrifices when necessary, and feel proud that such sacrifice will bring our fathers, husbands, brothers, and sweethearts home the sooner to us.

Letters, Edward Avery, Major, RAMCT, Sydney. I see no reason why a very high percentage of enlisted men, those who are not likely to hear a shot fired, should be given the extra rations as servicemen. There are thousands of soldiers on full rations who are not doing one-third the amount of manual labour undertaken by the munitions workers and miners.

ANOTHER VIEW OF THE YANKS

When American servicemen took their recreational leave, they usually flocked to the cities, and behaved as well as you might expect young unattached males away from their families to behave. Many of them were billeted by welcoming families, and they seem to have been on their best behaviour. At the other end of the spectrum, many others spent much of their time in pubs and night clubs drinking, wenching, and punching. Some of these met local girls, and by now a fair number had tied the knot, and taken unto themselves an Aussie bride.

In all of this hurly burley, the young men, with tons of spending money, in superior uniforms, and the lure of distant places, were often seen as dashing and captivating by our young lovelies. But adventure often has an unhappy side, and this unhappiness was now beginning to show up to this innocent nation. So that **criticism** of the infidelity and cupidity **of the young American visitors was becoming widespread**.

Still, sane voices, speaking on their behalf, could be heard. **Letters, H Gilchrist.** Intelligent people agree that sane education on sexual relationships is desirable. But it seems to me that, in the handling of the present campaign, much more discrimination should be used. The "young-girl-found-with-soldier" angle has been played up so strongly that we get the impression that the majority of Servicemen (especially American) are predatory wolves in khaki, while most schoolgirls are budding Delilahs. There is a tendency to concentrate upon and over-emphasise one aspect of a nationwide social problem. It is high time the Serviceman and his sweetheart were given a break. Australians, who have had tens of thousands of their own menfolk overseas, should be more generous in their criticism of the American soldier.

We of the AIF were received in South Africa in WWI with open-handed hospitality, entertained, and admired by both sexes and went on our way greatly heartened by an emotional send-off. In Great Britain, we were treated like Royalty and every home was open to us. The Digger's popularity was assured, and he spent as lavishly and courted as successfully as his Allied cobbers do in this country today. In the Middle East barriers of language, race, and class kept us confined to our own society, and it was then that the longing for a glimpse of decent home life became acute.

The American serviceman, too, has travelled thousands of miles to offer his life, if need be, in the common cause. I fancy he is as grateful as we were for whatever home comforts we can offer. That he finds the majority of Australian girls as sweet and wholesome as the ones back home I have no doubt. The critics would do well to save their spleen for the Japs and give the fighting men, the decent girls, and Cupid a fair go.

Comment. Quite a few girls had already gone to America as war brides. Some of them settled in well, with some it was too early yet to tell, and quite a few had returned home with sad stories about their mothers-in-law and their own unrealistic expectations. This two-way traffic grew over the next few years.

DOBELL AND JOSHUA SMITH

The Archibald Prize was given each year to the person judged to produce the best portrait. The perceptions of would-be judges differed greatly, so there was always some controversy over the choice of the winner. This year however, the prize went to William Dobell for his portrait of Joshua Smith. It provoked a furore centred on whether or not the painting was in fact a portrait, and not a caricature. The end-product of Dobell's work was not at all a faithful depiction of how Smith really looked, but rather an image distorted by the adventurous artist.

The morning after the prize was announced, Smith's parents begged Dobell to withdraw it. Smith refused to talk to Dobell. Dobell was strongly criticised in some quarters, including a wealth of abusive mail. Under the pressure, he suffered a mental breakdown and retreated to the shores of Lake Macquarie, near Newcastle, where he lived till his death in 1970.

We will return to Dobell and his painting of Joshua Smith later in this book.

OTHER MATTERS

News item. The RAAF educational services have produced for the WAAF a useful booklet called "Make It Yourself." It contains simple rules for the guidance of the amateur dressmaker and many hints on the preservation and repair of uniforms.

Air Force girls are being encouraged to make new clothes from old. "Make It Yourself" contains practical suggestions for making frocks, jackets, skirts, shorts, blouses, and underclothing from old topcoats, suits, evening dresses, or outmoded day dresses. It tells by diagrams and simple instruction how to take measurements, adjust a pattern, cut and fit, and give garments a neat, attractive finish.

It also shows the airwoman how to make extra collars out of the tail of her blue shirts or to turn frayed or worn collars, and it gives useful little hints on removing stains, pressing, etc.

Letters, Bahadur, Queenscliff. Australia has a small population of some seven millions, India of 366 millions. To afford worthwhile relief to India's "teeming millions of starving citizens" (by immigration), we would need to allow hundreds of thousands of Indians, if not millions, to migrate here. The numbers that came would not only increase of themselves, but gathering pressure would be exerted from India itself for more and more migration. It is hardly conceivable that any Australian would wish to see his country filled with migrants at a tenth the rate that fecund India could supply them.

Indians are worthy people, thrifty and hard working, but the masses have perforce a low standard of living. If paid a lower wage in Australia to correspond with his home standard of living, the Indian would monopolise the labour market to the exclusion of Australians. Indians are land-hungry people and notable small-holding farmers and traders. The North Queensland Italian would rank as a mere amateur alongside an Indian in the matter of acquiring land. Australian land-holders and small traders would quickly be menaced – and I mean menaced – by these would-be migrants.

As for defence, it is instructive to remember Mr Gandhi's policy regarding the Japanese menace to India itself – **a policy of non resistance, if not active collaboration**. Whilst Mr Gandhi does not represent all Indians, it is true that he inspires the All-India Congress Party, which is the most articulate voice in India. If such an influential body as Congress should not oppose what is

surely the cruelest and most Imperialistic attack
ever launched by man, then by what process
of reasoning does anyone deduce that Indian
migrants to this country would rush to the defence
of Australia?

Finally, Indians are intensely nationalistic, and
where-ever they have migrated, they have presented
the local administration with a first-class political
headache. Such could not be otherwise here. I
have much liking and respect for Indians, and
have learnt to respect their intelligence and good
qualities.

The complex questions of colour, religion, and
racial differences have purposely not been raised.
I am not one of those who consider a dark skin
inferior to a fair one, but I do vehemently believe
that it is best for both that they should not be
mixed.

Comment. An example of our White Australia Policy as
it was then.

A WARNING ON BOT-FLIES

Letters, William Crisp. Max Henry, commenting
on my letter, condemns my theory, but in the next
sentence admits he knows nothing concerning the
disease. With all due respect to Mr Henry, I still
claim that the cause of the whole trouble is the
bot-fly. In a case on Jimenbuan Station, in the
Monaro district, 50 years ago, my brothers and
I, after careful searching, found the maggot had
actually made his way through the bony pipes
in the nostril until it had reached the casing of
the brain, the casing for the site of a two-shilling

piece was eaten away until it was as thin as tissue paper; then the casing was pierced when the horse became blind, and mad, and acted as though trying to climb the stockyard fence, and at other times trying to push the fence down. From the time he began to act peculiarly until he died was less than two hours.

NEWS FROM THE BATTLEFIELDS

Over the course of January, the Russians had won victories on a battle front that extended from the Baltic Sea down to Ukraine and the Red Sea. They had now occupied parts of Poland, and were within 30 miles of Estonia. To the south they had occupied parts of the Ukraine and, in the area of Leningrad, were encircling vast German numbers.

In Italy, the Brits and Americans on more-or-less separate fronts were advancing north and, at month's end, were 13 miles from Rome. In the air, they were gaining more and more superiority. Look, for example, at these numbers. On 30th January, 2,000 planes attacked Berlin and Frankfurt, and dropped 5,000 pounds of bombs. You probably do not know what the tonnage of bombs means, but let me tell you that if we were at the same time bombing the Jap base at Rabaul, we would drop about 100 pounds. So 5,000 pounds is a lot of bombs.

Australian troops in New Guinea were continuing their winning ways. It was a slow, hard slog, and many wondered **later** whether it would have been better to just leave them there, in their isolation, to rot. But at the time, it seemed the right thing to do, and the Aussies were doing it well.

In all, the war was going as well as any war could.

FEBRUARY NEWS ITEMS

The Federal Government appointed Sir William Webb to **investigate Japanese war crimes against Australia**. Full details of any violations, and the names of those perpetrating them, will be submitted to the UN War Crimes Commission for record and punishment.

Doctors in the fighting forces may now perform medical services for **civilians,** under an amending regulation issued by Canberra.

On the Russian front. February 6th. About **130,000 German soldiers** have been encircled and **are being systematically wiped out** near Kiev **in the Ukraine**. It is the biggest enemy disaster since Stalingrad. Moscow says that, though the Germans are fighting fiercely, they have little chance of escaping.

For having **sold wine at greater than the official maximum price**, a restaurant proprietor and a waitress were fined 50 Pounds and 20 Pounds respectively in the Special Court.

Identity cards should be carried at all times, the Director of Manpower reminded. Regulations require that cards must be shown to any on-duty constable, or Manpower officer.

Manpower officials yesterday "raided" **large queues** at morning sessions of **two city theatres**. This was part of a drive to **check identity cards.**

A lorry got out of control in Kogarah when **a gust of wind struck a deflated gasbag on the roof** of the vehicle. The driver was killed.

The seller of a second-hand car at above **the fixed price**, in addition to being **fined** 100 Pounds in the Special Court yesterday, was ordered to **refund** the surplus payment.

The **Country Women's Association** said that since the start of the war in Britain, they had made **27,620 sheepskin vests** for the RAAF, the RAN, and the merchant navy. **Fantastic.**

A Western Australian tramway-man was fined four Pounds for **keeping a pig in his bath.** The pig was left on his tram by a passenger. The Lost Property Office would not accept it, so he took it home and kept it in his bathroom until he could find the owner. He failed to do this, so he took it on his bicycle to a piggery. Neighbours, who had seen the pig, notified the authorities, and they prosecuted under the Health Act.

Authorities for two years had been urging citizens to **save paper.** They had set up an extensive system that involved the collection from households by a network of vans, and then **re-cycling.** Currently, people were hoarding large amounts of paper for months, and ringing and writing to authorities **begging for its collection.** All to little avail. The authorities were silent in the face of much criticism. **Did we still need the re-cycled paper?** Had we ever needed the re-cycled paper?

HERE IS THE OVERSEAS NEWS

Every day, the *SMH* produced a **Page-one Table** that summarised the news items from overseas. It gave **full details** of these stories on later pages.

Over ninety per cent of these stories concerned the war. They came from all parts of the globe, but heavy emphasis at the moment was on the conflicts on the Russian front and in Italy. The Pacific also starred. No matter **where** they came from however, they were rich in hyperbole, with the Allies always having **effortless** victories, over an enemy that was suffering more and enjoying it less. Apart from all the exaggeration, however, the basic facts remained true, that is, that the Allies were continuing to have great successes, and that it seemed that the writing **might** be on the wall for the Axis powers.

In any case, I have included a typical Table taken at a random date, February 1st, as an example of what our citizens were reading each day. I suggest you do not concern yourselves with the detail of what was going on, but rather just browse the mixture of items to get some idea of just how widespread the war was geographically, and what devastation it was causing throughout the world. **And what our citizens were reading**.

Russian spearheads are less than 13 miles from the Estonian border in their spectacular drive to block the German retreat from the Leningrad front.

Red Air Force bombers, flying ahead of the retreating Germans, are attacking troops and supply trains between Kingisepp and Narva.

The Russians are silent about the southern front, but the Germans report big Russian attacks in the Dnieper Bend, resulting in battles comparable with those in the north.

Berlin Attacked. The total tonnage of bombs dropped on Berlin since November was brought to 20,000 tons on Sunday night, when RAF heavy bombers again attacked the capital, for the third time in three days.

Since Thursday about 7,500 tons have been dropped on German cities by Allied bombers. About 4,500 tons have been rained on Berlin.

When large forces of United States heavy bombers attacked Hanover on Sunday, they and their fighter escort shot down 91 enemy fighters, for the loss of 20 bombers and five fighters.

RAF Typhoon fighters shot down 12 enemy aircraft for the loss of one during offensive operations over northern France on Sunday. Warrant-Officer J Stanley, of Bondi, accounted for two Focke-Wulfs.

Italian Campaign. The latest Allied communiqué says that the Ansio bridgehead is being steadily supplied, enlarged, and strengthened as the troops already established ashore fight their way inland and fresh troops and supplies arrive.

On the main Fifth Army front on Sunday, American tanks and infantry captured heights beyond the Rapido River bridgehead north of Cassino.

Hitler's latest speech. London commentators agree that Hitler's latest speech shows that at last he is convinced the German people need realism as a tonic and, therefore, he let them know the Reich's grave position for the first time.

TOBACCO "RATIONING"

The amount of tobacco and its products available to citizens had halved by degrees since the war started. Some of this had gone to the men in the armed services, and some more had gone to the men in the CCC. Then again, nearly all of it came from America, and shipping from that country was always dubious. Pilfering by wharfies, and the subsequent sale on the black market, also kept the wheels of commerce turning. In any case, tobacco was in short supply for the man in the street.

However, it was not formally rationed. In those days, tobacco products were not sold by infants in Coles and Woollies, but rather through tobacconist shops These latter people knew their customers, and who smoked what, and so they introduced an informal system of rationing. This was supposed to simply limit purchases to all customers by the same percentage amount, so that everyone would suffer a similar deprivation. Of course, there was no chance that such a fair system would actually work, and instead "favouritism" ruled the roost. So some smokers got almost nothing and others got a lot, at a price.

Complainants became most vocal every time the suppliers turned the screws. Below is a small selection of Letters protesting about faults in the system.

Letters, LLL. Why must tempers of workers be frayed by tramping from shop to shop for cigarettes or tobacco, when cable news reports that there is no shortage in England, and statements by travelers that New Zealand has supplies to meet demand? The Minister for Customs has said that there is a limit to the output of manufacturers, because of insufficient female labour. Cigarettes could be sent out to retailers in cartons of, say 5,000, and the saving in cardboard and cellophane would be very considerable.

Letters, Pensioner. The Minister for Customs has stated that **alien prisoners of war** receive three ounces of tobacco and cigarettes a week. At Deewhy, Collaroy, Narrabeen, Randwick, Balmain, and other centres there are eventide homes conducted by various religious denominations who admirably cater for returned soldiers of previous wars, fathers and grandfathers of boys fighting in this war, men of the merchant marine, captains of industry, and others too numerous to mention, who in the past have done Trojan work for their country.

There are **hundreds of pensioners in these homes,** and it is pathetic and disgraceful to see these poor old fellows hobbling about (some on sticks and crutches) from shop to shop trying to purchase a bit of tobacco, only to be told by the shopkeepers that their quota is sold to customers before they receive it. Surely one shop in each locality could be supplied with a sufficient quota to enable us to purchase three ounces a week (on production of identification card) and thereby place us on an equal basis with our alien prisoners of war in this respect.

Letters, L S W. Practically all tobacconists show a sign from the first to the last day of each month that they have no cigarettes or tobacco, though one must assume that these shops get some supplies.

Surely a better distribution could be arranged than one where special people get what they want and others get nothing. As a taxpayer I should be entitled to my quota of supply and some arrangement for individuals should be made.

SERVICEMEN'S WIVES

Some of our young girls were falling for American GIs, and marrying them, and perhaps then migrating to the USA. At the same time, other girls were finding that their men-folk being away was leading them into **adventures and liaisons** that were not in keeping with the expectations of their men in the military. Inevitably, a number of **"Dear John ...." letters** were being received. The pain felt by the distant soldiers is evident from these Letters.

Letters, Chaplain (C of E), on active service overseas. There is much talk, and occasional public comment, on the behaviour of a proportion of the wives of men on active service. One who is by the nature of his duties much in contact with this problem cannot but remark the lack of an effective public opinion on such matters.

It would be ridiculously wrong to think that the proportion of misbehaving wives is large, however hard it might be to estimate, and it must also be true that some would have misbehaved in any circumstances, but it is generally agreed that there is a number, small in proportion, no doubt, who would not have misbehaved if war service had not removed their husbands from their homes.

It is difficult to describe adequately the suffering of the man who learns, while serving overseas, that his wife is unfaithful. Most often it is not possible to give a man any hope that he will be able to get home to try to set things right. There are too many men with good claims of all sorts. Probably most men take such troubles to a chaplain fairly soon, but in other cases, and these are significant, they come to light when a commanding officer is puzzled by a series of offences or failures by a man who is usually sound.

If this aspect of the problem were realised more widely, it seems unlikely that the general reaction would continue to be merely casual scandal-mongering, as now. Persecution or ostracism after the fact would be entirely wrong, unchristian; but a genuine public opinion before the fact would surely make a great difference. Nobody can do more to help a man on active service than his wife, and it follows very plainly that she plays a tremendous part in the common cause. She should consider herself and be considered in that way at need. She should have what she does not now receive, the effective practical moral support of a sound public and home opinion.

Letters, H Cosier. Having served both in the ranks and as a chaplain during the last war, I can support the statement of your chaplain correspondent. Loyalty of the women at home is a man's greatest comfort, and the news that they are unfaithful is bitter disappointment. It is for them that he fights. May it be suggested that **attendance at public worship** would strengthen the lonely, tempted women. In God's house is found the grace that revives the dying fires of love and loyalty.

THE CLERGY IN THE WAR

Letters, A Crawley. I am dismayed by the types of sermons we are getting from our priests. Apart from notices early in the sermon about fund-raising activities for the war, the war itself rarely gets a mention.

Week after week we get the same tired sermons we have had about the New Testament and Jesus and the so-called real meaning of such-and-such a parable, but no mention of the great turmoil going on around us. No one wants a sermon talking about the military aspects of the war, but we should be getting directions and thoughts about morality, tolerance, hatreds, dealing with suffering, sin in our new society, and the like. But we do not get this. It is as if there is no war going on.

There were a lot of people who agreed with Mr Crawley, but it was easy to find evidence that **his experience was not matched everywhere**. The Monday morning Papers all devoted several columns to what leading churchmen were talking about, and while a half of them suggest Crawley's comments were correct, the other half show a greater willingness to face the current issues.

For example, right now one issue raised from the some pulpits was what should be our attitude to (Italian) prisoners-of-war **here** in Australia? **On the one hand**, there were those, often with personal experience gained overseas, who hated them and wanted the harshest possible conditions for them. **At the other end of the spectrum**, there were those who saw them in full Christian light, and thought they should be regarded now as harmless, and be given the same rights as other aliens.

Others saw them as workers who could be employed as farm labourers (as indeed many of them were), **while others extended** this and welcomed them as possible future migrants. Mr Crawley's argument was that in most Churches, such issues were shied away from.

Bishop Duhig in Brisbane was not shying away. He had something to say on war-time morality.

News item. A strong attack on social evils arising from the war was made by the Archbishop of Brisbane, Dr Duhig, in a Lenten pastoral letter read in Queensland Roman Catholic churches yesterday.

The present war-time has been remarkable for a growth of sexual vice that is one of the ugliest blots on the fair name of our country. This evil no longer hides it head in secret. It has boldly emerged from its dens and hiding places, and stalks brazenly through the streets of our cities, where vulgarity has almost completely ousted the courteous and gentle manners of bygone times.

While mothers and little children seek in vain for a place on which to lay their heads, luxury and immorality, able to pay high price, can find ample housing accommodation where young girls are nightly lured into habits of drinking and dissipation that rob them of chastity and honour, and leave them wrecks of their former selves.

This is not an attempt at drawing an imaginary picture. It is, alas, only too true, and the public authorities seem powerless to cope with it. Vice today is being commercialised, and men are growing rich on its proceeds. Toleration of sexual vice has grown into a grave scandal. This evil tendency can be **met only by early religious training.**

The people need a united voice to tell the civil authorities that they disapprove of houses of ill-fame, and that, if they continue to exist, it should be made a criminal offence, subject to severe penalty, to receive in any such house any young woman under 25 years of age. We should give no quarter to soft living, but insist on moral self-control for our youth, and on victory aided by God's grace over low inclinations which, if unchecked, bring shame, humiliation, and foul disease.

Dr Duhig said that the **scourge of birth control** had left its scars deep in Australian national life. "The day might yet come when it would prove to be Australia's complete downfall," he said.

Letter, Tom Battersley, Manly. We are daily confronted with our politicians steadily taking away our rights and trying to set up a socialist state. After the war, we will be confronted by a society with all the regulations in place, and no way of getting rid of them. That is, a full socialist state.

Our clergy have great privileges in society. They are able to sermonise to large audiences every week. They can raise issues that need to be raised. But, time and time again, they do not. They hide under sermons about love of God and other platitudes. If Christ was here, he would have lots to say about the world we live in, and would have been a strong advocate against the evil influences in society. But his spokesmen, the clergy simply ignore all of this.

So the clergy, for example, are silent on the rapid growth of socialism. I don't care if they are for it or against it. What I want is for them to speak out with courage on such issues. To take a stance, or present fair arguments on the matter. They should be bringing such matters to the forefront of debate, instead of pretending that the love of God will somehow make them go away.

A REFERENDUM IS COMING SOON

By the end of February, it seemed certain that the Labour Government was going to put a referendum to the people soon. It thought that the nation should be planning for life after the war, and that the strict control of people, production, prices, profits, rationing and most things was the way to go. **That is, being Labour, it was opting for a socialist state.**

At the moment, various laws had been operating that allowed it to interfere in all of these matters, but they were set to expire, generally six months after the end of the war. The Labour Government of the day did not want them to lapse, and would soon formally propose a referendum that would give them the powers that they wanted. This was a strong proposal, t**o change our economy from a free-enterprise capitalist society to a controlled socialist state. Permanently**.

The first two *SMH* Letters put the case **for**, and **against**, in a nutshell. There will be others as the referendum gets closer.

Letters, A Huie. It seems to me that Government grossly exaggerates its need for further powers. According to Mr Holloway, they are faced with the problem of finding jobs for the vast majority of the men and women who were either in the Services or doing direct or indirect war work. I have been assured that the proportion really needing some help is only 30 per cent.

I cannot imagine a worse method of dealing with after-war employment than a great extension of Government administration. Have we not been plagued with countless examples of incapacity through the administration of sub-governmental authorities, boards, commissions, committees? Give the Government greater powers, and this huge, inept system of over-government will continue indefinitely. Those who lived through what followed the last war will not vote for further centralisation of powers.

So far as I can see the Government wants to follow the lines adopted after the last war on a more pretentious scale. They led to wasteful expenditure on works and closer settlement, a boom and a depression. The Government has sufficient power already if it will be wiser this time and avoid the mistakes after the 1914-18 war.

Letters, Edward Masey. At the end of the war, we shall be faced with the problems of (a) finding peace-time employment for over one million men and women now engaged in war activities.

Then, (b) preventing a huge rise in prices, due to inflated spending power arising from large war-time earnings coupled with an acute shortage of goods.

And, (c) preventing a short, sudden boom, created by the abnormal demands for goods now in short supply, to be followed by a slump beside which the 1929-34 depression would be inconsequential.

Finally, (d) disposing of our major primary products and maintaining our rural economy in the face of huge carry-over of wool, together with the competition of artificial fibres produced by gigantic chemical plants seeking outlets, and a devastated world unable to pay fancy prices for our foodstuffs.

The Commonwealth Parliament has no power in peace-time to deal with these problems. Surely our correct attitude should be to arm ourselves with the constitutional machinery to cope with our problems, and to see that it works without abuses.

MARCH NEWS ITEMS

In Britain, the Archbishop of York has suggested the use of "reconcilers" to help **husbands and wives whose marriages are endangered** by long separation caused by the war.

Manpower defied. Of the 80 women **directed from small shops** to a month's work in two Sydney canneries, **only 30** started work yesterday. Within the canneries, there were 90 **absentees** from a work-force of 500.

Current requirements for **entry into Sydney University** demand a pass in **a foreign language** in the Leaving Certificate exam. From next year, this will no longer be required.

The Federal Minister for the Interior has arranged for admission of **a half-caste lad from the Northern Territory to Queensland University** to undertake an engineering course. The costs for his fees and maintenance will be met by the Feds.

All travel between Britain and neutral Eire has been banned. This is designed to reduce the amount of military intelligence that is allegedly being passed from Ireland to the Axis powers.

Australian Servicemen **will be permitted to wear a stripe** on the left sleeve for each wound received.

The Electoral Commissioner of NSW has reminded people that **posters** for State elections are limited under the National Security Act. **The maximum allowable size is 10 inches by six inches.** This applies "on land, on the water, and **in the air**."

The first woman enrolled with the Women's Australian Auxiliary Air Force **(WAAAF)** three years ago today. This was nine months before the Japanese invasions started.

The scale of war. An American air fleet of **1,700 aircraft**, and **a strong fleet of RAF heavy bombers**, gave Germany no respite on Saturday from its continuous pounding. This was the fourth heavy daylight raid in four days.

Dr Evatt, Acting Minister for Supply, said that **25,000 hot water bottles** would be made available to the public, via normal supply channels, soon.

Mr David Selznick, film producer, told the New York News that **the gross takings of the film Gone With the Wind had so far totaled 25 million dollars**. Half of this was paid to MGM for lending Clark Gable to Selznick for the production.

The Minister for Trades and Customs said that special stipendiary magistrates would be appointed in all States to **hear black market cases**.

Five negroes of the US Army have been **sentenced to death** for the rape of an American Red Cross worker in Australia.

Italian men resident in Australia, and not naturalised, at the beginning of the war were interned early in 1942.

They had been sent to farms to work, or sent to enclosed camps, depending on their behaviour. Now **most of these persons were released.**

A boy, aged 2, whose throat had been cut, was found in a house in Botany in Sydney. His mother was found nearby, with his young brother, aged 11. Both of these had cuts to their throats, and were weak from loss of blood. A razor was found nearby.

The Government announced that shipping space might soon be found for **a large accumulation of books** that were being held in Britain, ready for export to this nation. **Until now, no space had been available for them.**

Reports of **Japanese atrocities on prisoners-of war** were flooding in from all over the Pacific. The Australian population was growing even more angry at the Japs.

Buildings, in the form of camp huts, hospitals, and warehouses, which would stretch **end-to-end for more than 120 miles**, have been pre-fabricated by the Allied War Council of Australia by mass production methods. They are for the use of the US Army in Oz and the south-west Pacific.

A Department of Commerce official said that consideration was being given to **reducing the butter fat in ice cream** to make more cream available for use in making butter. Australian ice cream uses several thousand tons of butter fat in ice cream per year. He added that he had eaten British ice cream without butter fat, and it was "quite palatable"'

NOT EVERYONE IS HAPPY IN EUROPE

The Russians had won spectacular victories on all fronts throughout the month. In the North, they had closed in on Poland and the three Baltic States of Latvia, Lithuania and Estonia. Down in the south, they were pushing on the borders of nations like the Ukraine, and Romania. To the Brits and America, and also to Australia, this was great news. The Hun was being put back in his place.

Not everyone, though, was completely happy. Those small States mentioned above were in a quandary. They certainly wanted Germany to be defeated, but they were now getting apprehensive about the advancing armies of the Russians. Every one of these States was now occupied by the Germans, but they all had governments-in-exile, mainly in Britain. These were composed of political figures who had fled their country ahead of the German occupation, and had been given asylum in their new host nation. They had formed new "National" Governments and were recognised as de facto representatives of the interests of their nation of origin.

With the Russians advancing close to or into their home territories, these persons were now anxious to get control of their homelands, and to keep these lands safe from what could become **a new invader, namely Russia**. Everyone knew that the Germans would not retreat without a great fight, so it was inevitable that the Russians would come to occupy the entire nations. Could this be done in such a way that once the Germans were permanently gone, the governments-in-exile could return and take over as controllers of a sovereign nation? Or, and this was the current worry, would Russia simply stay put, and install perhaps a puppet government, and become the effective ruler of the nations.

So, at the moment, all of these little powers were seeking to get some promise of good behaviour from the Russians. Most of them were having "peace" talks with the Reds, discussing such matters as where their boundaries with Russia would be, and how persecuted minorities would be treated. As it was turning out, **Russia was taking a hard line** with these smaller States, and was not willing to compromise its future actions by agreeing to restrictive peace treaties with them.

The matter was very much in the air, but with the Russian armies advancing day-by-day into the various States, with no one prepared to hinder them, the **prospects for a happy peace were quite dim for the little States.**

ENOUGH REGULATIONS TO GO ROUND

The Oz world was now half-way to a socialist state. One sign of this was the endless proclamation of restrictions on business and people and the issuance of endless and petty regulations. You might have thought that, with the war at the stage that had been reached, **relief from the regs** might have been the order of the day. You would have been right in a few cases, but it seemed now that the bureaucracy was getting a second wind, perhaps preparing for the socialist state that might come with the end of the war.

In any case, these bureaucrats, locked away from reality in Canberra and in the heart of the State capitals, continued to pour out regulation after regulation, in the vain hope that there might be someone out there who would understand them, and find a practical way to implement them. In my earlier *1943 book,* I produced statistics that showed the number of **Statutes** introduced by the Federal Government since the war started was 820, and that there had been **2,350 new Regulations**. Also, it had opened 14 extra new Departments, and all of these figures were matched by **similar activities by the States**. I must add that those figures covered the period up till January, 1943, and there has been a full year's growth since then.

To give you a feel for the cupidity generated in this field, I will give you an example of the regulations just issued for women's stocking and anklets.

News item. The Prices Commissioner gazetted **maximum prices** for all types of women's stockings and anklets. They are: Size of foot, 8½in to 10½in, full fashioned: Rayon hosiery, 6/9 a pair; mercerised cotton (lisle), 7/; all wool, 6/6; wool and rayon, 6/6. Circular: Rayon hosiery, 3/6; mercerised cotton (lisle), 3/9; all wool, 4/1; wool and rayon, 4/1. Anklets: All wool, 2/5; wool and rayon, 2/5; soft cotton, 2/-; mercerised cotton (lisle), 2/9; soft cotton and rayon, 2/1; mercerised cotton and rayon, 2/7.

There were **other prices for different sized feet**. There was no provision for where the sales were to be made. After all, a retailer in Alice Springs might expect to get a different price from one in Melbourne. There were rules for every other sort of stockings. In all, the regs were **another minor nightmare for retailers.** They also knew from experience that **these prices would change**, and new regulations would be issued, in a few months. They knew, too, that there was a host of inspectors lurking round every corner who would be delighted to catch them selling at the wrong price.

Still, the bureaucrats and their hordes of officials were happy in their jobs and, incidentally, were all **protected** from call-up provisions. Nice work if you can get it.

NO CHILD LABOUR HERE

Australia was lucky at this time to have **some** parliamentarians that gave them plenty to talk about. These were gentlemen who were all quite intelligent, and who were sometimes described as mavericks, and who had their own ideas that were sometimes regarded as adventurous. At the Federal level, Eddie Ward and Arthur Calwell, in their different ways, fitted this description. Sometimes, Doc Evatt, brilliant though he might be, also measured up.

As it turned out, Doc Evatt had a brother, Clive, who was by now the **Minister for Education** in NSW, and who at times had bright ideas that seemed a bit "different".

News item. The Minister for Education, Mr Clive Evatt, has directed a reduction in the homework given to pupils in schools under the control of the Education Department. He ordered that third and fourth class students could be given half an hour's reading from the school magazine, or to practice spelling or write poetry. This should be only three nights a week. He went on up through the classes, until he got to third year in high school and above. At that stage, home study was to be limited to one and a half hours, four nights a week, with much of it set as non-written work. No week-end work was to be given.

He added: "I am not going to permit the health of school children to be undermined by excessive homework. In some cases it has been established that physical and, indeed, mental breakdowns among children have occurred through too much enforced homework. This must cease."

These rules were to apply to his domain, that is to **public schools only.** In working out how much homework should be set, teachers were required to cater for "the average pupil, or even the slow pupil". What the bright kids were to do with their spare time was not stipulated.

Evatt went on to say that the regulations were binding on all teachers in the Department. He said that the instructions had been very carefully drafted, and the views of experienced teachers had been obtained.

There were many people who were aghast at this direction. They and their children had their ambitions, and knew that gaining entry, to places like universities, was really tough. Who among these good folk would give up homework knowing full well that their opponents would not?

In any case, Letters poured in. Most of them, though not quite all, deplored Evatt's idea.

Letters, Parent. If the principals of the State High schools carry out the Minister's order, and limit the amount of homework for third, fourth, and fifth year students **to what the slow boy can do in an hour and a half**, they are simply **making a present** of the large majority of passes in the Leaving Examination, and of all the best passes, carrying honours, bursaries, scholarships, etc, **to the student at non-State schools and colleges**.

The Minister seems to be moved by intuitions, always of course from the right quarter. So far they have as completely failed to achieve their objects as Hitler's have failed on the Russian front.

I have a boy in his fifth year at High School, whom I would very much like to see reach the University this year, and on first reading the absurd ukase, I was much perturbed.

I reflected that the State High School headmasters know more than the Minister does about this.

Letters, Parent. My child is in his Leaving Certificate year; he is neither brilliant nor dull. He is in good physical form, and tackles every job with good will. But he has quite literally not **one moment of unregimented leisure** between half-past six o'clock in the morning until half-past ten o'clock or later at night. Around what centre does our whole education system revolve? Surely around the child. Do schools, teachers, examiners, ever think of the child, or only of "results," of the school's reputation, of the respective claims of "subjects"? I agree with the Minister that children have too much homework. **When can they be carefree children?**

Letters, Another Parent. When James Garfield, one-time President of the USA, was a university student he had a rival. At exams, this rival invariably came out ahead of Garfield, who resolved to know the reason why. So he watched. Their rooms were on opposite sides of the quadrangle, and Garfield noticed that his rival's light was burning long after he had put his out. That decided the coming President. He resolved to study each night 15 minutes longer than his rival. This he did, and very soon the exam positions were reversed. There is a lesson in this for High School students. If third, fourth, and fifth year scholars let up on homework, it means making a present of the majority of examination plums to non-State and Roman Catholic schools, and I'm sure their students and masters will be quick to exploit the position. The measure of the success is the measure of the effort.

Letters, 5ᵗʰ Year Student, North Sydney High School.   Mr Evatt sounds all right in theory, but in practice we have found that it is just "a lot of bunk." I'm stating the case of hundreds of fifth year students of average intelligence when I say that we have at least three and a half hours' homework each night, a great part of it written work, and that is not including the extra individual study which must be done. This homework has to be done **in order to get through the amount of work prescribed in the syllabus** for the Leaving examination.   Maybe Mr Evatt can tell us how to get through the work which previously required three and a half hours' home study in only one and a half hours.   School children fully realise how badly the homework evil needs reform, but if the Minister wants **to reduce the homework by half then he must reduce the syllabus by half also.**

Letters, Tom Brown.   I wonder who the experts were that Evatt consulted.   He refused to name them or even give some sort of description of them. Were they from this century? After all, homework was unheard of 100 years ago. Then again, they could be from people with no chance of having children. They would have no knowledge of the dog-eat-dog world, for university spots, out there. Clearly, Evatt has no knowledge at all.

CENSORSHIP

The Oz Government was as diligent as ever at stamping out the flow of useful information to the enemy. As was their standard practice, they were **over-doing all aspects of this**, and filling the Courts with silly charges, given that the battles of the war were being fought many miles from our shores. Never-the-less, letters to and from our Servicemen were all likely to be censored, even if they were posted to relatives and lovers. At the same time, servicemen were not allowed to write to newspapers, perhaps expressing grievances, and the news and opinions that the newspapers could publish were under close scrutiny. Likewise, radio stations were controlled. Remember, we were constantly being told. "Careless talk costs lives".

So now, over two years since the war started in Oz, the various censorship bodies suddenly started **to extend** their spheres of influence. **Up till now**, letters from **Civilian A to Civilian B** were not opened and scrutinized by the censors. But **now** that there **was almost no chance that any info that these persons had would be of use to the enemy**, out came their letter-openers, and **citizen-to-citizen mail** was being read.

Men in high places reacted against the new procedure. Influential Federal politician Spooner and the Editor of the *SMH*, for example, both thought that it was "Gestapo-like." They thought that it was arbitrary to select only some Letters, and wondered about how they would be chosen. Would the Letters of certain politicians be opened? Would the Letters of certain political Parties be somehow always selected? Would Communists get more than their fair share of attention?

Both of these gentlemen went on to question why it was that the new form of censorship was being introduced at this stage of the war. Surely, they argued, it was now appropriate to **remove some of some of the censor's role**. The *SMH* said that if there was indeed a need, then it should be exercised only with the specific approval of a Court order.

Mr Spooner cited the case of a young woman who had written a letter to her boy-friend in the Army. In it, she had "bragged" (her words in court) about performing an act in a factory that was "not productive". This Letter was opened, and **she was charged on the basis of the letter**, despite her claim that there was no truth to the letter. Spooner argued that this was a denial of fundamental freedoms and that, in private correspondence, she should be free to write as she chose. If she wanted to brag in a private letter, or tell untruths, or theorise, then she should be free to do so, without the heavy hand of the censor telling her what to write. He concluded that "what is at issue here is the right to send communications passing from one person to another which have no relation whatever, by even the wildest stretch of the imagination, to the security of the great country."

From Letter-writers came a volume of indignant mail. The Letter below is typical.

Letters, R Malloch. One of the grandest traditions in Australia's history is the sanctity of the letter-box, whether it be in the city, the village, or the remotest outback. As a youth raised in the country I can recall the withering contempt expressed by drovers, squatters, teamsters, and even "sundowners", for the swine who pillaged a grazier's letter-box.

The wide, open box or kerosene tin attached to a gumtree or gate-post, often many miles from the addressees' homestead, would be easy game for those with the looting instinct, but to the everlasting credit of the plain people of the outback, pillaging was, and still is, I believe, a rare crime.

Against this wholesome background one recoils with horror on reading your report of the ravaging of private letters by high government officials – for other than security reasons. Not for half a generation has the confidence of the community been so deeply shocked as by the revelations of the Prime Minister and other members of Parliament concerning their private letters.

IS SOCIETY GOING TO POT?

Almost daily, reports were appearing in the newspapers of raids on two-up schools at scarcely-hidden venues round the nation. It was clear that the police knew about these schools, and raided them every now and then to keep the record up. The players, men and women, were always paraded before the courts, and given trivial fines, and in all seriousness, exhorted to avoid vices in the future. Many of the men now-a-days were on-leave servicemen, and had plenty of spending money. Some people argued that this "vice" was not a "true vice" but only an inevitable activity for young men bent on having a high time. They said that the only vice really was the corruption of the police force, and the consequent reduction in respect for the law.

In any case, the Minister for Customs warned drinkers of the dangers of drinking any non-reputable wines.

"Bombo" and "hooch," he said, were being sold on the black market, and the possibility that **the distribution of such poisonous liquor had been organised by enemy agents was being investigated.** Examples of bad liquor, he continued, found in recent weeks by the "Keane-Evatt black market liquor squad" included:

Inferior wine, attractively bottled and labeled, which contained scores of small house flies.

Another bottle, described on the label as "very fine old" sherry, in which a lizard 2½ inches long was "pickled."

Brandy contaminated by phenol, the result of using corks from bottles of sheep-dip, according to the distributor.

"Consumption of this poison has caused scores of Servicemen to go AWL, we believe," Senator Keane said. "Allied Servicemen have been admitted to hospital in a serious state after drinking wines manufactured in irrigation areas."

Some aliens, responsible for thousands of gallons of the stuff flooding the Sydney market, **were suspected Fascist sympathisers**", Senator Keane said.

Another MP gave out a different warning. A Mr Turner said in the Legislative Assembly that "two-up, drinking, and women were the only diversions of many Australians who left school at 14. The educational system gave these Australians no other interests." He urged the establishment of part-time schools where children above school-leaving age would be required to attend to develop personal interests, talents, and hobbies.

Mr Turner was directing the attention of the House to a "notorious" two-up school in his electorate, which, he said, was conducted nearly every day in the week because the law was ineffectively administered.

He added that because no attempt had been made to administer it properly, the law was brought into contempt. The two-up school in his electorate was about a mile from the station, and most of the patrons came from the city.

"Everybody makes a day of it," Mr Turner said. "They boil the billy in the bush. There is a parking area, and a large iron shed in case of wet weather. There is an iron galvanised shed for the caretaker, a nicely-swept ring, and fixed rustic benches."

Two-up was not a peccadillo, he said. Games in the Middle East had had serious results, and some soldiers had sold rifles to Arabs because they had lost their money at two-up.

"The formal education obtained during school years was hardly sufficient to found those interests without which people turned to two-up, drinking, and other rather worthless occupations."

HOPEFUL NEWS FROM JAPAN

In Japan, people were getting uneasy. For example, comments such as this on Tokyo Radio were becoming more common. "**Some Japanese say that they are getting tired of the war**. Such people should **remember that they are in danger of an air attack**, in which, if it is comparable to the attacks on the Marshall Islands, their homes would be completely destroyed."

LET'S MAKE SOCIALISM PERMANENT?

The Government said it was considering t a **referendum** to give it powers to run a controlled economy **after** the war.

To its supporters, mainly its Labour voters, the idea of a more socialist State was a good one. After all, the economic progress made under such a command economy was obvious to all during the war. **To its opponents**, mainly non-Labour voters, the price that the whole community had to pay was too high. The restrictions and regulations and bureaucracy inherent in such a system was abhorrent to them. **I will come back to this referendum later.**

Here, I point out that the newspapers were opponents of the referendum, and wanted it to fail. As it turned out, the action over the *Daily Telegraph*, and its result, **did a great deal to educate the population of the dangers of having governmental control over aspects of life.** Whether the timing of the newspapers' action was deliberate or not, it certainly helped to bolster their case against the proposals in the referendum.

APRIL NEWS ITEMS

A force of RAF bombers, "attacking Nuremberg in very great strength", lost **96 planes in the raid**. This is the RAF's highest loss in a single night's operation, the previous total being 79 on February 19.

Grafton Municipal Council, in coastal-country NSW, will be the **first Council in the State to establish a free public library**. About 25 other Councils are doing this..

Vi Withers has **set a world record for cutting and pitting peaches** for canning. In less than 9 hours, she treated 100 boxes of peaches, an average of over 12 boxes per hour. Each box contained 50 pounds of peaches.

In Britain, a spiritualist medium has been sentenced at the Old Bailey **to nine month's imprisonment on a charge under the Witchcraft Act.** Helen Duncan "pretended" to recall the spirits of deceased persons from the dead. In effect, **she conducted séances.** She remains the most sought-after spiritualist medium in Britain.

Under the heading of **"Boy Basher Gangs"** in the *SMH*: "Special plain-clothes police are endeavoring to put a stop to the activities **of gangs of boys in Sydney suburbs**, Paddington and Darlinghurst."

In NSW, there were 3,814 petitions for **divorce, restitution of conjugal rights, nullity and separations** last year. **This was an increase of 1,444 petitions over 1939. Divorce** petitions increased from 2,379 in 1942, to 2,978 in 1943.

A man and a youth were swept off **crowded trams** by passing trams in Sydney yesterday. The condition of the man, who lost his arm, is critical.

The Army will reduce its numbers by 90,000 this year. The Army Minister, Frank Forde, said that Australia must **plan** for **a population of 30 million in the next 30 years**. In fact, 70 years later, the population had reached 22 million.

"Wonder," **the talking budgerigar**, died this morning at the home in Woy Woy. He was featured in a film, now showing at battle stations, and made 140 Pounds for war funds. At the age of three months, he could recite **"Little Jack Horner" in full**, and at nine months had **a vocabulary of 300 words**.

Although still legally a minor, Princess Elizabeth, who is **18 years old today** (24th April), could now, if the occasion arose, **succeed the King with full legal powers.**

The Government will examine **removing some forms of clothing control.** This follows on from **New Zealand abolishing men's austerity suits.**

The third year of rationing will start on June 5th. New ration books must be collected on June 3 or 4.

New item, April 30th. Daylight Saving in Australia has probably gone permanently. It is understood that although the fuel savings resulting from it are substantial, majority opinion in both Federal Cabinet and Caucus is that the hardships caused by it outweigh its benefits.

NEWS FROM THE BATTLE-FRONT

There were two stories that need telling. **Firstly, in the Pacific** the Allies were making good progress. To the north-east of Australia, there are chains of multiple islands, such as the Solomons, that the Japanese had invaded and occupied. The Allies, particularly the American fleet with its many aircraft carriers, were now attacking these, using what is sometimes known as island hopping. This means that they attacked some of the bigger concentrations of the Japanese, but ignored the others. So that Jap soldiers on many islands were "left to rot", with very few ships and supplies getting through, and with no replacements, and with no one to fight. This policy of using the US fleet to attack here, and then there, was proving most effective, and the Japs had no answer to it.

Secondly, in Italy, the Allied forces had ground to a halt about 50 miles from Rome. They had landed easily enough at **Anzio** a few months earlier, but had delayed moving forward. This had given the Germans time to settle into defensive positions, with the result that Allied attempts to advance had been stifled. So Italy remained in a state of turmoil. The north was occupied by the Germans, and Mussolini was supposedly running the government there. The south had been overrun by the Allies, and Italian leader Badoglio had set up an administration that was recognised by them. But in each of these regions, there were, among the ordinary citizens, Fascists, and anti-Fascists, and Communists, all of whom hated each other, and many of them were bent on sabotaging whatever administration they were under. Something in Italy had to give.

One final point here. The Russians had continued their massive victories against the Nazis, and their rate of progress appeared to be increasing. It seemed that nothing could stop them. The only doubt for the Allies was in India and Burma, but even there it seemed that the Japs **might** have run out of steam. **There**, time will tell.

THE VOICE OF THE MIDDLE CLASS

At this time in Australia, the middle class consisted of doctors and lawyers, and pharmacists, and shop-owners and bankers and a few public servants. These were people who had never joined a trade union, had never gone on strike, and who never got paid for overtime. If you looked at them **in 1941**, most people would have thought they were in an enviable position. They were running their own businesses, which supposedly gave them a good safe income. They could work their own hours, and the longer they worked, the more money they got. Many of them had cars, their kids were well clothed, and they had their own bungalows. This was pretty good at the time.

Since then, the position had changed. I will not dwell on this here because I will let the middle-class make their own points in Letters in a few minutes. But let me say that while the working class was now receiving wages boosted by war-time rates and overtime, the middle class was not. **The prices they could charge were fixed by legislation**. As well as that, much of their office and clerical aid had been taken away by Manpower and the Army, so they were chronically short-handed. Their cars were useless without petrol, and their kids scarcely got enough coupons for decent clothing. In short, while the working class had never been richer, the middle class were being badly squeezed. I leave it to them to tell you all about it.

Letters, E C, Sydney. I am one of the new poor, and in their interests I write. We are professional men, business executives, higher Public Servants, and others of the like who, for moderate reward, accept positions of trust for our fellows and oil the wheels so that the world rotates smoothly for the big mass of the people. Years of midnight oil and much personal self-sacrifice brought us to our present positions.

Now we are the new poor, benefiting little by the enhanced earning power of the general mass of the people, but providing a particular target for the tax-gatherer and for every bureaucrat there is.

Take my own case. Before the war, when my insurances, house-payments, and other fixed charges were in reasonable adjustment with my earnings, my aggregate annual taxes were about 80 Pounds. My current assessment has now reached 490 Pounds. My income remains practically unchanged at pre-war level, and all fixed charges which represent my family security go on as before, so I face a 750 per cent increase in taxation, apart altogether from the rise in living costs.

Now the Prime Minister and the Treasurer calmly appeal to me to invest in the Victory Loan, with implied suggestions of bad faith if I fail to do so. In point of fact, I have not one single war bond. Long ago I had to sell my earlier bonds to pay my taxes; now my wife's bonds will have to go as well to meet Mr Chifley's later exactions.

Even this attempt at domestic financial equilibrium is achieved only after eschewing most of the amenities which average families regard as rudimentary. Expenditure in my household on liquor, smokes, and gambling is nil, on entertainment negligible, on clothes and luxuries the irreducible minimum. Thus, after a lifetime of industry and good citizenship, my reward is to be one of the new poor, with little prospect under the regimented future being prepared for me, and no desire to encourage my offspring to follow in my footsteps. Why should they, when a paternal government will relieve them of the necessity both of thinking and exerting themselves? There are many like me – the forgotten toilers of the middle-class; so vital to the maintenance of our community life, so little regarded by those in authority.

Letters, Middle-class Man. While this condition of disequilibrium persists, there can be no hope for members of the middle class – unless, of course, they consolidate their forces in political action. They are there at present for the asking of any party prepared to provide them with a decent deal.

Letters, Middle Classer. As Mr Menzies said, "they are unprotected and uncatered for." The vocation of the professional man is jeopardised, in some instances to the point of extinction. What may an architect do today, but seek a Government job, or enter a new vocation? What may a builder do? His men are dispersed, and his opportunity to use his skill and ability in building much-needed houses is restricted. What may a solicitor do today? His chief business is conveyancing; and conveyancing has been almost totally extinguished. The Federal Government has restricted the free sale of property. Consequently, buyers are off the market to a large extent.

Labour is organised. The great middle-class is not, and what it must learn is that a rabble can never exercise its claims in the face of organised opposition.

Letters, H Walker. It is fortunate that your correspondent, "Middle Class Man," has forsaken the normal attitude of his class, and become articulate. He has been exploited for many years, but never so shamelessly and cynically as during the war period. Usually the child of parents not well off, he is educated at considerable sacrifice, and acquires a profession, business, or trade in the same way. With thrift and enterprise, he may achieve a modest competence, and avoid that which he detests above all things, becoming a charge on the State.

There is no class in the community with greater loyalty, higher ideals, or more self-reliance, and it is these traits which have made him an easy mark for political parties like those in power at Canberra and in Sydney. His loyalty induced him to vote for a Government which "would get on with the war," but he thought that meant, among other things, **making miners, slaughtermen, wharf-labourers do some work.** His self-reliance has kept him out of pressure groups, for he is an individualist, and dislikes politics.

"Middle-class Man" suggests his own answer in his last paragraph. Self-preservation demands that his class must consolidate itself in political action, and it was for just that purpose many, including myself, became members of the Democratic Party, whose policy he will find caters for the good of the whole community including the "Middle Class Man."

Letters, Walter Bunning, ARIBA, Sydney. The true position of the middle class is becoming clearer with the development of monopoly capitalism. Many small businesses have been swallowed up by the monopolistic octopus, and their owners have become employees. Many of the monopolies are **employing their own professional men on a salaried basis.** A Government salaried medical service appears to be a distinct possibility.

With the change in status from small employers to employees, these professional men are finding their institutes, while having a part to play as learned societies, are employer's bodies and therefore no longer represent their interests in the economic field. Therefore, many salaried architects, engineers, and other scientific workers **are joining unions**. They realise that better economic conditions represent a recognition of ability and the improved status means a better opportunity to use their knowledge. Other sections of the middle class should learn from the lead of these professional men, and realise that they are **an important part of the working class**, and that their interests lie together.

Contrary to "Middle Classer's" insinuation that an architect accepting a Government job suffers "extinction," many architects are welcoming the opportunity to lend a hand in the real development of this country, in the housing, national and public works, and so on, rather than cramping their knowledge by merely satisfying the whims and fancies of private clients.

THE DAILY TELEGRAPH IN THE NEWS

For over two years the Commonwealth Censor, backed up by censors in the States and the Army and other bureaucracies, had been enforcing a strict censorship on the public as best as it could. Newspapers and radio stations were also controlled, and this had resulted in quite a few more-or-less public brawls between the censors and the various forms of public media.

In mid April, this antagonism boiled over. Two weeks earlier, the Press across Australia reported that many frustrated newsmen from America were going home, and many others were refusing to send their copy to America. The reason given was the Australian censorship was far too severe, and was preventing them from telling a true story to the world.

At the same time, the war was receding further from our shores, and most people thought that it was now time to reduce interference with the flow of information. After all, the whole idea of it was to prevent important information coming into Japanese hands. Surely now the official inspections and interventions could be materially reduced. But only last month, the censors had started intercepting private mail, from one citizen to another, and it seemed like the system was being increased rather than reduced.

In any case, and whatever the immediate cause, the *Daily Telegraph* in Sydney was on April 16 pushed too far, and decided at last to push back.

On that Saturday, the *Sunday Telegraph* was being readied for print, and it contained four small articles that were critical of Government policies. The Department of Information, with the active involvement of the Minister Arthur Calwell, ordered the paper to delete the articles. The paper did that, but **left vacant the space that they would have occupied**. In total about 20 column-inches, spread over Page one and Page three of the paper were set with empty rectangles. Needless to say, they were quite conspicuous. Mr Calwell told the paper it could not go to print like that, and ordered the *Telegraph* to remove the rectangles. The *Telegraph* refused to do this, so the Censors sent police to the offices of the paper, and seized all the printed versions of that day's papers, except for a thousand that had been dispatched earlier. So there was no *Telegraph* available with breakfast on that Sunday morning.

All hell broke loose. Mr Henderson, head of the Australian Newspaper Association, became spokesman for the Papers. Arthur Calwell was spokesman for the various censorship bodies. Henderson issued a five-page letter that set out the complaints against Calwell, which had been central to the confiscation of Sunday's papers. In it, he gave many examples of articles that had been recently censored, and promised that many more were available. **The thrust of the letter was that censorship was, in many cases, directed towards the political objectives of the Labour Party, and protecting its Ministers from criticism and**

slighting remarks. It was not, as it was supposed to be, an instrument for protecting the nation from enemy actions at all. It was being used as a political tool, that was suppressing comments and information that **had absolutely nothing to do with the war situation.**

For example, he cited suppression of comments on a tram strike in Melbourne, on the appointment of Mr Casey to a position in India, on our immigration policy, and on the reduction of crippling dust in coal mines. In no way could this info be considered to be any interest to the Japs. He pointed out that Calwell had repressed comments in the Press on himself, to the point of triviality. For example, he had struck out references such as "Calwell, the Nazi Minister for Misinformation" from the record of a speech given publicly by Alderman Aitkins from Townsville. In all, Henderson's letter emphasised the fact that censorship was often directed to internal political purposes.

Calwell replied in his usual pleasant manner, with the uncensored view that Henderson was inaccurate and untruthful and the Australian newspapers were engaged **in fifth-column activities.** So, the battle of words raged. Calwell went on to **suppress Monday's edition of the** *Daily Telegraph*, **and Monday's edition of the** *Sydney Morning Herald.* When Henderson sought to get his letter out on radio, Calwell again suppressed it. Calwell went on to issue charges under National Security Regulations against almost **all of the major papers on the east coast and South Australia**, charging them because of their editorials on the whole matter.

THE HIGH COURT STEPS IN

By Tuesday, the High Court of Australia had heard various injunctions, and issued orders **restraining** the Commonwealth Government and the censors **from endeavoring by any means to prevent publication of articles and editorials relating to the censorship imposed over the last few days.**

The effect was that papers could go about their business in the normal way.

But conflict raged on. Let me give you just **two examples**. **The first** was a dispute involving the NSW Police Force. After the papers were confiscated on the first occasion, Calwell issued a statement that said **the State police** had stopped the circulation of the papers. To most people, the interference with the freedom of the Press was regarded as abhorrent, and any police force that participated in this was to be condemned. So the NSW Police set the record straight and pointed out it had been **the Commonwealth Police**, so called "peace-officers", **who had enforced the restraint**. The Premier indignantly backed them up, and so the matter devolved into a nasty fight between Calwell and NSW Police, with recriminations lasting for weeks.

The second example of the effects of the conflict was that the Letters to the *Herald*, and other newspapers, were not published for over a week because the matter had come "before the Courts". There were many, many Letters received by the newspapers condemning the censors' and Calwell's actions, but it turned out that these Letters were suppressed by the censors, because the matter was sub judice. This was very convenient for the Calwell camp, but it hardly advanced the cause for free speech.

THE HIGH COURT'S SUBSEQUENT ACTIONS

The High Court sat on Thursday and Friday, and the following Monday. By then it had sorted out the major issues. There were **two of these**. **The first** was whether the censors had acted correctly in intervening, given that **the items prohibited did not seem to relate to national security in any sense?**

The second issue was whether the censor had **the right to suppress** publication even if the matters were **not** of national importance? Calwell's argument was that the National Security Regulations simply gave the Censor the right to close newspapers, **if he chose**. There was nothing in the regs that said just what the cause of suppression should be, only that the censor had the right to interfere if he thought that he should. That is, regardless of whether valuable information was going to the enemy, the Censor had **the right to close newspapers simply because he thought they should be closed**. This argument was clearly against the original legislative intent, but because of the way that the regulations were written, it seemed to have some validity in Court.

The matter was adjourned until early next month, and so we will wait till then to watch for further developments. Let me point out in the interim, that tempers were not soothed, that barristers and solicitors were licking their lips at the prospect of the coming barney, and that newspapers, sensing that some changes to censorship rules were in the offing, were quietly relishing their positions. But their problem was that no matter what they thought, they were still afraid to speak their mind because Calwell could still use the power of the State to suppress anything they said.

WHAT'S FOR DINNER, MUM ?

Mum probably does not know yet, but she will be getting the feeling that cooking will be a lot easier in the future. That is because the new gadgets now available overseas will be on sale in Oz. These include electric stoves and bonzer electric toasters. Something to look forward to.

KEEP AUSTRALIA DRY

Home brewing of beer for domestic use and for sale on the **black market** was widespread, the Minister for Customs said today. Prosecutions would be launched against all persons found manufacturing the stuff. **Ignorance of the law would be no defence.**

DON'T FORGET THE STRIKES

Strikes are still with us. For example, 900 workers at the Dunlop Rubber Factory in Drummoyne in Sydney went on strike today as a protest against the Rationing Commission's decision **to grant** them **each one ounce only of tobacco every week.**

MAY NEWS ITEMS

Speculation is growing in Britain than an **invasion of the European continent might occur soon**. The preparation for such an event would be a mammoth undertaking, and it is inevitable that some news of it would leak out. Such news is the basis for much speculation.

Also, in Europe, troop movements indicate that **the Germans are re-enforcing a number of regions around the French and Dutch coasts.** This is adding to the feeling that the Germans too are expecting an invasion. Germany's Marshall **Rommel** told his commanders that he regarded an attack on Europe western front as likely **in the next few weeks.**

Princesses Elizabeth and Margaret saw an opera for the first time last night when they accompanied the Queen to the New Theatre where, from the Royal Box, they saw the Sadlers Wells Company in **"La Boheme."**

A Melbourne magistrate ruled that the word **"copper"** **was highly insulting to a policeman.** He imposed a fine of two Pounds for the offence. The magistrate said that the defendant, who was a public servant whose duties brought him into contact with the police, should not have used the expression **"only a soft-headed copper"**.

May 12th. A young soldier was **stabbed in the abdomen** in a brawl in Darlinghurst last night. His condition is grave. Three US negro soldiers **stabbed a man** in Sydney yesterday morning and threatened two other men. **Comment:** Such incidents were common in the drinking areas of Oz cities.

Manpower will check on Brisbane dwellings occupied by **women not gainfully employed**. It expects to find numbers of women who could be put to more useful work.

One in every 340 homes in Australia had **a Service member in Japanese hands**, statistics show.

Many soldiers on leave in Sydney are asking police to give them a bed **in cells** because **they cannot get proper beds elsewhere**.

In addition to the release of imported **hot-water bags**, more **rubber will be released** for local producers.

In Britain, Mr Eden told the House of Commons that 47 British and Allied officers had been **shot dead** when attempting to **escape from a German prison camp.**

Since **US troops** have been in Australia, **2,500 officers and men have married Australian girls.** The girls retain their status as Australian citizens.

The War Cabinet has decided that no more zoot suits will be allowed till further notice. (See my 1943 book).

Any form of dancing should be forbidden by the Church, a speaker at the NSW Presbyterian General Assembly said yesterday

A SECOND FRONT COMING IN EUROPE?

Early in May, the Allied forces launched a very positive attack **in Italy**. They had previously been bogged down for a couple of months along the Gustov Line, but now they had advanced beyond that and were attacking the so-called Adolf Hitler Line. They had momentum, and the defending Germans seemed to be in major disarray. The immediate target of this push northwards was the city of Rome. I will give you an up-to-date account at the end of the month.

In Britain, the place was a-buzz with expectations that the Allies would soon land ground forces in Europe. This view was supported by the enormity of the air attacks on Germany and its satellites, every day and every night of the month of May. Hundreds of planes, sometimes thousands, took off twice a day and pounded the enemy everywhere in Europe. On top of this, large numbers of planes were being launched from southern Italy, and north Africa, and Russian bases, with the idea of crippling Germany. Surely, this was a softening-up-for- the-invasion process.

Back to Britain, and there the movements of troops and the fact that troops were confined to their barracks at the end of the month seemed pretty good indicators. If you needed a further broad hint, the Archbishop of Canterbury came out with this injunction.

News item, Dr Temple, Canterbury. All those who have charge of parish churches and other places of worship should be available for prayer from the time the news of the opening of the second front is received. They should be ready to lead services of intercession, and dedication, and to lead great congregations in prayer on the following Sunday.

Comment. The Archbishop was part of the Establishment, and would not have issued his direction without advice from the Government. So, here he is, in effect, telling the Nazis that an attack was imminent. **But they knew this anyway, more so than the British people.** He was just stirring the pot, with the hope that the more info the Germans got, the more they would spread their troops round the shores of western Europe, and not guess correctly the when and the where of the invasion.

ARE GERMANS GOODIES OR BADDIES?

This is a question that was constantly raised in 1944, and in all subsequent years. Was the current war simply a result of Hitler's exploitation of the desire of the common folk for a better deal from the Allies? Did they want what was clearly justice for themselves, and had they been hoodwinked by Hitler and the Nazis into following a false prophet? And now was it too late to change?

Or had Hitler been able to thrive because he represented forces of evil that were deep inside people who were filled with hate and the desire for revenge? Were they seeking the glory of conquest, of domination, and the persecution of other races not measuring up?

The Editor of the *SMH* had no doubts on this matter, and expressed them in no uncertain terms.

There are many misguided sentimentalists in both Britain and America, as well as in Australia, who still pretend the Nazis are an inoffensive, peace-loving people who would never have followed Hitler unless compelled by force. They claim that they have always been in sympathy with the democracies, and they are only waiting a chance to rise and destroy their hated regime.

But this is not the true situation. The whole German soul is shot through with a megalomaniac lust for power. They are pitiless disciples of blood and iron when the word is given from on-high.... Their propagandists today are putting out the suggestion that the fault is all that of Hitler and the Nazis, in the hope of averting punishment once again, as they did after 1918. The Germans whined then that they were ruined by the reparations demanded, when, in fact, they collected loans and credits from the victors four times the value of Germany's cash payments – and then defaulted on the lot.

The Germans' glorification of force and fraud has risen in a steady crescendo since Frederick the Great's days. Hitlerism is only the current representation of German aggression.... Not only should the whole German nation be indicted, but the victors cannot avoid indicting it. There has been no protest from the German masses against the wholesale massacres, the horrible slavery of whole peoples. There has been no reluctance among Germans to share in the loot.

THE *DAILY TELEGRAPH* IN COURT

By early May, the lawyers and barristers had taken over in the newspaper dispute. There were no more wild statements from politicians, and none from the newspaper lobbies. It all became very sedate, with every word carefully considered. The High Court sat a few days, adjourned a few times, heard a number of approaches, and never got down to real legal issues. It did order the Government not to seize more papers until May 21st, and then it suggested that this was a matter for mediation and conciliation, and after a couple of weeks, the parties went into private discussions, without the guiding hand of the High Court.

Still, all of the hush-hush light and harmony was only on the surface. There were many bitter feelings between the parties, and occasionally they slipped out for the public to see. For example, the newspapers on May 10 published the official closing message from the Australian Newspapers Conference.

News item. This conference representing all the daily metropolitan newspapers in Australia views with grave anxiety the extent to which censorship has been used for purposes entirely unrelated to security.

It declares its unreserved acceptance of censorship designed to prevent the disclosure of any matter of military value to the enemy. **But** it is convinced that any attempt to use censorship to maintain morale by suppression as was done in France in 1940 is wrong and dangerous and that any further effort to distort or limit reports of industrial disputes is contrary to the public interest. The conference believes that the knowledge that such matters are subject to censorship will destroy public confidence in what is published and therefore declares itself irrevocably opposed to a continuance of such practices, and this conference fully supports the action of certain newspapers in challenging political censorship even to the extent of suffering suppression in order to uphold the principles of freedom of expression within requirements of national security.

This one must have just squeaked through the Censors, given the circumstances.

So, under the cover of High Court, civility, and the measured processes of the law, **the battle raged on a number of fronts.** In the long run though, the parties did emerge from their conciliation meetings, on May 19th ,with the matter hopefully resolved.

They announced that the dispute between the Government and the newspapers had been settled, and a code of censorship principles governing the powers of the censors had been gazetted.

News item. Under these regulations it is provided that censorship shall be imposed exclusively for reasons of defence security and shall not be imposed merely for the maintenance of morale or the prevention of despondency or alarm. Censorship shall not prevent the reporting of industrial disputes or stoppages. Criticism and comment, however strongly expressed, shall be free.

Except in case of immediate and obvious danger to defence security, a breach of censorship directions shall be dealt with by prosecution, and not by seizure of the proposed publication. In any Court proceedings following a seizure, the onus of justifying the seizure will rest on those responsible for authorizing it.

This was a result that **completely validated the actions of the newspapers**, and left Calwell and the Government with egg on their faces. Everyone was too civilised to comment much on it. The result spoke for itself and there was no point in exulting, or scowling, publicly. **The newspapers never did publish the hundreds of Letters that they received** but could not print at the time. They **could** have published them at this time, but obviously thought it was better to not gloat and kick the cat.

RANDOM COMPLAINTS AND SOLUTIONS

The ordinary persons in the street were at this time pretty well adjusted to the war-time economy. Despite all the problems that faced them in their day-to-day life, they realised that all their privations had a point to them, and that while ever the war continued, they would suffer them. **But they were not disposed to suffer in silence.** Grizzling was one great art perfected in the war years, and it was rife in the pubs, in the shopping queues, in the factories, over back fences, in the army, the homes, and in the newspapers. So, I have presented here a few good grizzles, sent to *SMH* Letters by people who had got so fed up that they actually **did** "write a Letter to the Herald."

Letters, Parenta. My daughter, young, in perfect health, a champion pea-picker, answered an advertisement last week to pick cotton. She wasted three half-days away from work, ten shillings in fares, only to be rejected as too tall. Why not advertise for short girls only to apply?

Letters, M Stollery. I agree with Mr Lamb that useful horses should not be destroyed. In 1934 there was over-production; wheat could not be sold at a profit because of the high cost of running and maintaining tractors. Banks at that period were prepared to advance money for the purchase of horses, but would not make advances for the purchase of tractors. Horses, which, until then, had been a "drug on the market," became very popular and, as they were scarce, high prices were paid for them and buyers travelled long distances in the hope of purchasing suitable animals.

The "Herald" had this to say of a horse sale held in Goulburn in 1934: "Buyers were present from Sydney, Wagga, South Coast, Temora, Young, Moss Vale, Riverina, Braidwood, Crookwell, and Taralga. Prices: Unbroken draught mares, 3 and 4 yrs, to 40 Pounds 10 shillings; unbroken draught fillies, 25 Pound to 35 Pounds; broken-in draught mares, 30 Pounds to 40 Pounds," etc.

Quite recently, 350 horses, mostly draughts, were sold at Orange. Dog-butchers offered 2 Pounds each for them. Why are horses being discarded? Has the false prosperity of today deluded the men outback into the belief that they can with safety return to the tractor and relegate their faithful servants, the horses, to the slaughterman?

Letters, Country Woman. Mr Makin promised the country people that dry batteries (for radios) would be available for all in February, but none have come to light so far. Now comes the news that the department has announced that the batteries will be available within six months. With the long winter nights ahead, we are going to spend more radioless hours, but we can still keep on hoping that something will be done to relieve the situation that means so much to us country people.

Letters, Logic, Goulburn. Why is the Railway Commissioner unable to provide one day-time train for most stations south of Goulburn on the main Sydney-Melbourne line? The Riverina express runs every second day, but only stops at the main stations. If another train cannot be provided, the Riverina express should stop at all stations south of Goulburn. Under present conditions a trip of 15 to 20 miles has to be made to connect with the train, and yet we are asked to save petrol and tyres.

Letters, Harry Fentone. Isn't it about time something was done to stop the foistering on the public of the present so-called suitings? Those responsible for this poor quality should be removed before they meddle any further with the wool industry. If their idea was to stop spending of money they have fallen down badly. Instead of a man getting one decent suit to last at least two years, he has to buy about six of these rags or go naked. Considering the price of wool today and the small increase in wages a man should be able to get a double weft suiting made up for 10 guineas regardless of what the manufacturers say.

Considering the enormous damage done to our wool trade by the **numerous synthetic fabrics now on the market**, it is nothing but sheer stupidity to persist in foistering this parasitical material on the public. The same thing applies to the wool felt blankets. The smell of the dags still adheres to this latter rubbish, together with various grass seeds for good measure. **Botanists** may appreciate these blankets. They could spend many hours studying their science, if they should survive asphyxiation.

Letters, V M G. After reading "E C's" letter, I would like to introduce another forgotten and overburdened class, which is also hard put to it to maintain a semblance of their pre-war standards. I refer to the **wives** of officers and men of the active Services.

The pay on which we have to live is not increased accordingly with the sharp rise in the cost of living. In order to live within our pay, we can afford no one to help us with our children, at the fantastic rates that have to be paid these days. If we have no relatives to look after our children, we can never have a rest or a holiday. What is the use of the Government formulating grandiose schemes for increasing the population in the future, when the young wives and mothers of today are being reduced to nervous wrecks from over-work.

Letters, E Goulding. For a considerable time past there has been no information on postal pillar boxes, as to when the "next clearance" will take place, so that one posts mail in simple trust that the man has not yet been to clear the box, or later in the day, that one has not missed the last clearance. I never remember any explanation being given as to why the time signals were removed. Would it not be possible now to have the times of clearance exhibited once more.

Letters, Sufferer. If Senator Keane is so anxious to relieve the shortage among consumers of tobacco, he should abolish all quotas of tobacco to industrial canteens. As it is now, an industrial worker can purchase his regular weekly quota from the canteen and also augment his supplies from his grocer or tobacconist, and thus cause other consumers to go short. This shortage falls most heavily on farmers and land workers in industrial districts and the country areas.

Letters, W S Edwards. The building industry needs assistance from engineers, technicians, and industrial chemists who have provided a number of synthetic materials which can be cheaply produced, and which do not possess the defects of present building materials. A modern house still consists of one-third timber in spite of all defects of wearing and shrinking. There is no reason why steel should not be used for joists and rafting in fibro-constructed houses. The whole frame, including the roof, could be of fabricated steel. During the twentieth century almost all the large industries have been reorganised, but with the building industry, one of the most important in the country, the position is otherwise.

Engineering mass production methods are essential if we are to lower costs. In the Ford Willow Run Factory, huge bombers came off the line at the rate of one per hour – why can't we organise the engineering industries of this country **to produce a house per hour**? It can be done if the resources were utilised to that objective.

Steps should be taken to modernise the brick and tile industries, which are 50 years behind the times. We should install modern excavators and conveyors instead of picks and shovels and trucks pushed by man-power. We smile at the Arab's plough, but brickyards are just as ancient. Why do builders and Government authorities **insist on building houses to last three to four generations?** Compare the motor car of today with one 20 years ago. The engineers have given us a greatly improved car at a lower cost. The chaotic state of housing will not improve until modern engineering methods of production and planning are adopted right throughout the entirety of all the building industries.

THE FALL OF ROME

At the end of May, and in early June, the Allies breached the Adolf Hitler Line and poured into Rome. The Germans had agreed not to engage in street-by-street fighting there, so the Allies were able to enter triumphantly. On June 5th, **Churchill announced the fall of Rome in the Commons.**

From here, the Allies were pointed towards the mountains to the north, the Alps and the Himalayas. It turned out that these obstacles were almost impassible to an Army, and they were held at the foothills for months, until relief came from another direction. Still, they served their purpose, because they kept a large part of the German army occupied there, during the many decisive months just ahead.

THE REFERENDUM AND REGULATIONS

You will recall that I said earlier that there might be a referendum later in the year. The idea here was to cede some of the powers that the States had, and give them to the Commonwealth. These were in the areas of pricing, housing and wage fixation, for example. The stated aim of the Labour Government was to make the nation more efficient, and better **able to compete** with other nations in the post-war world. The supporters of this thought that such efficiency would be needed, and would propel the nation forward with little waste.

The opponents thought that individuals would have to give up many **personal liberties** that they had enjoyed before the war, and looked forward to getting back after the war. There was also the suggestion, from other quarters, that the same Labor Party might simply lust for the power over all aspects of life that socialism, on a grand scale, would bring.

All in all, it can be summarised as a battle of socialism versus free enterprise. And as the battle of the collective power of the State versus the freedom of the individual. And **even** as a microcosm of the battle of Russian Communism versus the forces of American Capitalism.

The date for this referendum had now been set for August 23rd, and even at this stage, the battle for success was being bitterly fought. It was likely that voters would be given 14 questions to either approve or disapprove, and if they **disapproved of one of them, the whole vote would be lost**. So that it was obvious that the Labour Party, who wanted the change towards socialism, would have an uphill battle. We will keep an eye on this as we get closer to the date. In the meantime, I will point out some factors that will influence the result.

JUNE NEWS ITEMS

Re the entry into Rome. American Press report. "One thing is outstanding. Rome has been left untouched. Citizens, in their Sunday best, pack the streets, waving flags and **welcoming the troops. It is a holiday.** Everyone is having a good time." **Comment.** Not everyone. The Fascists would have hated it.

The butter ration for all Australians **will be reduced** to six ounces per week, rather than the current 8 ounces. Five northern NSW coalmines were idle as a protest against the cut. The Federal Council of the British Medical Association (the representative body for Australian doctors) said the cut would adversely affect health, unless more fats were made available.

Six months after **production** started in Australia, the first **Beaufighter bomber** was handed over to the RAAF yesterday.

A Captain E Levi, a Jewish chaplain with the US army in the Pacific, pointed out that the economic life of South Sea Islands had been upset by the war. Before the war, **natives could get a good wife for one pig, but now she cost 40 Pounds in "good Australian cash".**

NSW has been flooded with **forged petrol coupons** in the last two months, officials announced.

June 16th. News item. German **crewless** planes, loaded with high explosives, were used in England today. They have terrific speed, with bright flames from the exhaust, and are crashed into targets. The engine of these "secret weapons" stopped, and 15 seconds later an explosion would follow. **It is probable that these attacks will continue.**

Civilian suits, in 100 patterns and 32 sizes, of the best material available, will replace **austerity suits** for discharged servicemen. Civilian hats and shoes will also be issued.

Artificial insemination. Three babies have been born in Britain after artificial insemination to which **a man other than the husband of the mother** had contributed, says Dr Margaret Jackson in the Lancet.

A woman was found dead in her home in Sydney's Marrackville, two days after the cottage had been **fumigated with cyanide** for rats and vermin.

One pair of **corsets** per year for every woman is the aim of the Rationing Commission, the Quota enquiry was told.

A witness at the Quota enquiry said that **unsuitable shoes** for women had caused the worst **outbreak of tinea** for 20 years.

Mickey Rooney has reported for duty as **an Army private** in California. He was inducted into the Army last March, but his call-up was deferred so that he could complete a film.

The life of a Perth airman was **saved by penicillin**, the **first time** RAAF doctors used the drug in New Guinea.

Of the **39,000 pairs of pyjamas received** from India, 10,000 would go to NSW.

For having **used the identity card of a dead man**, a Mr Lucas of Austinmer was sentenced to three months gaol in Bulli Court. The man had been dead for two years, and the card was used to gain a ration book.

Conscientious objectors to fighting in a war were **despised by many citizens.** They were often imprisoned, for a period of about three months, and on release, **were charged again, and imprisoned again.** By now, **some men were doing their fifth term in prison.** Some agitation was growing to better employ these men, by perhaps having them serve in the CCC. But there was **not much sympathy for them in the population.**

News report, 7th. **Police officers,** who inspected a painting at the Sydney contemporary art show, **did not uphold a complaint of obscenity.** Art-lovers were always **offended that it was the police who were called upon to make such decisions,** and they questioned what qualifications the police had to make them. **About 20 years later** the police, together with Customs officers, **still exercised much of this power.**

Bobby-pins will be back on the market in a few months, and all demand will be expected to be met by the end of the war.

D-DAY: THE INVASION OF EUROPE

On June 6ᵗʰ, 1944, a completely new phase in the war started. Allied forces, in a huge armada, landed en masse at five points of France's Normandy shores, and proceeded with establishing beachheads. They were supported in advance by 13,000 paratroopers and glider-borne troops, and backed up by non-stop bombings of enemy positions by aircraft. In general, the landings went well. The Allied navies pounded away with good effect at the enemies' coastal positions. Only on one beach, Omaha, did they suffer greatly, and there the Americans lost 2,000 dead before fighting their way inland.

Reaction in Australia, Press report. News of the invasion, which was electrifying the whole world, caused great excitement in Sydney.

News item. Toasts to success were drunk in all city hotels, and there was keen discussion in trams, trains, buses, and ferries as business people travelled home. Intercession services were held in a number of churches last night, and more services will be held today.

First news of the invasion came from German-controlled radio. Though this was treated with some reserve, it stimulated interest for the announcement broadcast later by the BBC, in which the Supreme Commander, General Eisenhower, told of the landing.

The BBC announcement had been forecast by local radio stations before 5.45pm, and when General Eisenhower spoke, hundreds of thousands of people were listening in. Cafes with wireless sets were tuned in and diners and café staffs listened together. At a King's Cross café, two French people wept openly when General Eisenhower referred to the French nation.

Audiences cheered and sang "God Save the King" with emotional fervour when news was read in several city theatres last night. The audience at the Tivoli rose in a storm of cheers when the English actress, Jenny Howard, interrupted the show to read news of the invasion fleet. The audience sang the National Anthem.

At the Theatre Royal, Maxwell Oldaker read the news. Audience and cast joined in singing the National Anthem.

From the time the first news flash came through, switchboards at newspaper and radio offices were jammed with calls from people asking, "Is it true?"

Within an hour of the announcement of the landing, leaders of all denominations had arranged services of intercession for the Allied cause. Services were held at St Andrew's Cathedral, St Mary's Cathedral, and some churches in the suburbs.

Dr W Wilson Macaulay, Moderator-General of the Presbyterian Church of Australia, said he was sure that everywhere churches would be open for prayer. He asked that prayers include not only our anxious desire for victory, but also that, if it be possible by the mercy of God, the time of trial should be shortened and the end be swift.

Over the next week. On June 14th, General Montgomery summed up the week. "We have won the battle of the beaches, and have a good firm lodgment area, which we can

use for developing our plans. I am very happy and pleased
with this situation. The violence, power and speed carried
us right over the beaches and miles inland very quickly,
except in the case of the American landing". He went on
to say that "the Americans, on landing day, had advanced
only 100 yards inland before evening, but are now 10 miles
inland. This is good news indeed. These troops are very
gallant, and very brave."

In Hitler's captured territories. German authorities in all
the **captured nations** in Europe imposed new restrictions
on the citizenry as a result of the Allied landings. In French
cities, for example, mass arrests of persons, suspected
of being pro-Allies, were made. All cafes, cinemas,
theatres, and restaurants were closed. The sale of alcohol
was prohibited. "Civilians may not ride bicycles or drive
cars. Assemblies exceeding three persons are prohibited.
No civilians are allowed on the streets at night-time. Co-
operation with the Allies is punishable by death."

At the same time, resistance movements were emerging
from the underground. Again, France provides a good
example. "**Patriots** in the far north are fighting a German
unit of 2,000 men, 300 of whom they captured." "50
locomotives have been destroyed in the area." It was now
reported that France's secret army, for weeks before the
Allies landings in Normandy, had dynamited railways,
attacked power installations, and destroyed several local
radio stations. In Yugoslavia, in particular, the patriots were
overtly active. A rebel Army, financed by the Allies, was
in open rebellion against the Germans, and was winning
notable victories. Everywhere across Europe, there were

hopes and expectations that the Allies would win through quickly. But these hopes were always hedged by the thought that the winning of victories would take a terrible toll, and who knew what price each individual would pay for his ultimate peace.

Sidelights of the invasion. I present below one of the many clippings **that always adorned the hard news in the papers. Far be it from me** to say that as I read them, I gained the impression that **they were probably all made up**, and that they were planted by **propaganda agencies.** So, I will not even mention that suspicion. But, **I will** mention that as I am writing this book, I do need to be alert at all times to the dangers of accepting any reported account at its face value. And that I need to check and re-check my so-called facts.

Anyway, I ask you to look at the three little stories shown here, and decide for yourself whether these were figments of well-meaning imaginations, or grizzly reports of real-life facts.

Our War Correspondent, Somewhere in France.

A sergeant and a private of a British unit were captured by a company of Panzer Grenadiers, who held them some hours without sending them back to headquarters.

Finally the prisoners realised that they were guarded by only three men. They throttled one, grabbed his revolver, shot the second, and brought the third back to the British lines as a prisoner.

A Scottish corporal, taken prisoner, submitted to search and questioning, but when he heard one of his captors call him an "English swine," the insult was too great.

He broke loose, clubbed his guards, and got away.

The third, a grim story, comes from a sector where every advance we have made has been dourly contested.

Infantry, moving into an area where the initial penetration had been made by a Commando unit, found in a slit trench the bodies of a British Commando private and a German private.

There were no weapons in the trench. Each had strangled the other.

THE REFERENDUM IS LOOMING

The regulations. While the Japs were in close proximity, everyone could see the benefits of the regs and restrictions. Now, however, the reaction against them was growing daily, and complaints about them were dominating conversations everywhere. The Letter below tells a tale of the frustrations felt by **doctors**.   Generally, such a person would not broadcast his problems to the world, but I assume he had gone past the point of moderate restraint.

Letter, A Practitioner. The general practitioner, due to the depletion of his ranks by the absence of colleagues on active service, has found his work increased to an unprecedented extent. At the present time he sees more patients in a day than in pre-war times he would have imagined possible, but for the most part he sees them cheerfully enough. He scarcely has time to eat, and his nights are seldom unbroken.

But the bane of his life is the necessity for providing his patients with certificates. It is not enough that he examines, diagnoses, treats, prescribes, advises, operates, and confines. He must certify for everything under the sun. He must use hours of time and reams of notepaper in order that his diabetic patients may obtain extra butter, his expectant mothers milk and waterproof sheeting, also pre-natal coupons and the maternity benefit.

No practitioner would grumble if it ended there. But it does not. Apart from these certificates he is expected to provide others – for hot-water bags and rubber tubing, for coke, gas stoves and frigidaires, rice, prunes and bacon, cream, for a special allowance of petrol where a patient must travel and is unfit to do so by train.

Many of these certificates are not accepted at their face value; the retailer of such commodities frequently rings up to ascertain whether or not the doctor considered their provision essential to his patient's health.

Regarding the recently introduced milk priorities, the Board of Health issued every medical man with a small supply of certificates and precise instructions as to which type of case merited a supply of milk and the amount per week to be given in each. With two exceptions such certificates remain valid for only one moth, so that if milk rationing is continued for more than a month, nearly everyone of these certificates will have to be duplicated, if not triplicated.

He is used by now to providing certificates for every patient of his who is, even for a day, incapacitated for work. The "works" must have one, the lodge, the sick club. In case of a long illness or convalescence following operation, few lodges or sick clubs are content with one certificate for a period of several weeks. They demand progressive certificates each seven to ten days. The doctor, who knows that his patient will not get paid his sick benefit unless he does, complies with these demands, rather wearily.

I have only one suggestion to make, and this is that the responsible authority in each case in which a medical practitioner's certificate is required – whether this be the Rationing Commission, the Milk Board, or individual suppliers of commodities in short supply – should make it absolutely clear, through the medium of the daily Press, to whom and for what reasons such certificates may be granted. This would at least avoid a large number of inquirers attending practitioners' surgeries, and would save the practitioner from the necessity of refusing certificates to patients who are not entitled to them.

This would also obviate confusion in the mind of the practitioner himself – he is often not clear as to who is and who is not entitled to a certificate.

It would also save him a good deal of useless writing if it were left to his discretion to state a time limit upon the validity of his own certificates.

Comment. A sorry state of affairs indeed. There is an equally sorry follow-up Letter a few days later.

Letter, Invalid. Even after doctors like "Practitioner" have filled all the forms, they may have wasted their time. I am unable to walk out of the house, and my doctor, in applying for an extra petrol allowance on my behalf, certified to and (after refusal) reiterated this fact. But my application was still refused.

Arbitrary Government decisions. The next articles highlight another area of grievance. That was the fact that Government made high-handed arbitrary decisions, and that only the most determined people could get redress.

For example, in early 1942, all boats such as launches or rowboats round the coast of Australia were seized by the Navy, and taken away. This was because it was thought that if the Japs arrived, they could make use of the boats. While the boats were in captivity, they were neglected, they often sank, and were often damaged. After about six months, the Navy said that owners could come and get their moored boats **themselves**, and it added that **no compensation would be paid for the damage and neglect** during their confinement. It also said that there would be no claims for **the cost of retrieving the boats**, which in some cases were moored hundreds of miles from their home berth. No one, to my knowledge, challenged these rulings successfully.

Comment.   A good example of the things a government can get away with during a war.

Another arbitrary decision. A long Letter described the travails of another boat-owner in his dealings with the Feds. Under the name of Fiat Justitia, he described how his vessel, the *Corrimal*, a cargo steamer of 1,970 tons, was impressed by the Navy in late 1942. By April, 1943, the Navy made him an offer of 10,000 Pounds, which he refused. After long legal battles, that went through several Tribunals to the High Court of Australia, that Court found in his favour to the tune of 32,000 Pounds. This was more than three times the sum offered by the Navy.

Comment. The *SMH* Editorial sums it up better that I can.

Editorial. Although the vessel was impressed in 1942, and later acquired by the Navy Department, it is only now, after prolonged negotiation ending in a departmental appeal to the High Court against an award of the Naval Compensation Board, that the owners have been awarded the value of their property. It is hardly to be wondered at that they refused the Navy Department's original offer of 10,000 Pounds, in view of the fact that the Court holds them to be entitled to three times that figure. In this case it has been worth while for the company to fight the matter before the High Court, and justice has been done; but most persons whose property has been taken over for war purposes must perforce accept the departmental idea of adequate compensation, even though they may feel that they have good reason to be dissatisfied. The Corrimal case is not the first of its kind to be brought before the High Court, and it is disturbing to find that such unrelenting judicial vigilance is needed if the owners of property acquired by the Commonwealth are to be paid or compensated "on just terms."

Comment. It was a bad time for public attention to be directed towards scrutiny of the Government's arbitrary rules and high-handedness. Every such complaint, publicly aired, seemed to be putting nails in the coffin of the upcoming referendum. Indeed it almost seems that the spate of such complaints was designed to do this. But .... no, no! Surely not.

ARTHUR CALWELL - STILL

When the High Court decided in favour of the newspapers in the *Daily Telegraph* case last month, I made the comment that "everyone was too civilized to comment on it much." It turned out that I was just a little bit wrong. In fact, if I might say so, I was **more than** a little bit wrong. If pushed, I suppose I would have to admit to being completely and utterly wrong.

I blame Arthur Calwell for this. I should have known that he would **not accept a High Court judgment against him** to be of any significance. I should have realised he would go away, lick his wounds and then return to the fray. That is exactly what he did. About the middle of June, amid a great deal of publicity and to-do, he went to the Labour Cabinet and proposed the introduction of **a new set of laws and regulations** that would fix the clock of the newspapers, once and for all.

He was backed up by the flamboyant Eddie Ward, and between them they proposed a seven point plan that **would have crippled the newspapers, and left them shells of their former selves.** For example, they proposed that the prices of newspapers be set at a low level that would mean they would have to reduce their staff to a fraction. They proposed that advertising rates be similarly cut. These suggestions were despite the fact that these prices had just been set by the Government's very own Prices Commissioner. In fact, **they were a clear and deliberate attempt to cripple the newspapers.**

They had more in mind. They wanted the CCC to go through **the newspaper offices**, and seek out men who could be drafted to work for the Army or CCC. Newspapers had already lost 40 per cent of their staff to the war effort, and now the happy couple were proposing to change the rump of the industry so that it was **no longer classified as protected.** All of the Editors would surely have gone. As the prominent Sydney journalist who summed up these facts said "Thus would the Australian Press learn that it doesn't pay to tell the candid truth about either Mr Calwell or Mr Ward."

The Cabinet threw out the proposals, and this time Mr Calwell did go quietly. Or at least, for a time.

Comment. It was widely said at the time that Calwell was unwise to continue his wars on various people, like the newspapers, and that he should learn to move on and get on with the job. It was a lesson he never seemed to learn, and it was one of the reasons many people said that Labour would never get back into power while Calwell was prominent.

Second gratuitous comment. My father also added, weekly, that Calwell had one of the best Labour minds of the **Victorian** era.

JULY NEWS ITEMS

Our Prime Minister urged that letters to servicemen should be **cheerful**, and not full of petty grievances.

Counsel for the Crown said in the Special Court that a skillful and daring **gang of forgers was operating in petrol ration tickets.** In the Court in one day, over 50 motorists were fined 1,050 Pounds for having the forgeries in their possession, and **one man was imprisoned for two months**

The Commonwealth Bank pointed out that it had created **special paper** to frustrate the forgers, but much of it had been stolen by the villains **before** it reached the Bank.

Petersham (Sydney) Council last night decided to **purchase rat poison for free distribution** in the municipality, and to employ **two rat-catchers**. It also decided to launch a publicity campaign concerning the rat menace by sending circulars to homes, and to institute inspection of premises.

Churchill announced that since June 13, **a total of 2,752 deaths had been caused in Britain by Germany's flying bombs** (doodlebugs). 8,000 persons had been hospitalised. Most of the victims were from London.

The Allies were developing air defences against the bombs, and were in turn **bombing German launching sites and the factories that made them.** He went on to say that the threat was of course serious, but would in **no way affect the progress of the invasion of Germany.**

American Flying Fortresses bombed several cities in Japan. "Japan's inner defence wall is being breached, and she must soon quiver, like Germany, under the power of the Allied air arm." So said a *SMH* Editorial. The morale of the Japanese citizenry tumbled to new lows....

Authorities in Tokyo have begun evacuation of school children from that city.

At mid-July, America had **7.5 million men enlisted in the Army and 4 million men in the Navy.** There were about 470,000 marines. This was the total for the European and Pacific spheres. It is expected that there will be no increase in this number.

According to Tokyo Radio, American airmen, who are **captured after bombing the Japanese homeland, were being executed**

News item, July 7th. **Thousands of women and children were leaving London.** The damage from **the doodle-bugs** has not been as great as the 1940-41 Blitz, but the regularity of bombing has become nerve-shattering.

In the middle weeks of July, **American Super-Fortresses bombed Japanese cities on three separate occasions**.

Also at the end of the month, there were **virtually no German troops remaining on Russian soil.** Hundreds of thousands of **German bodies** still lay about.

PILOTLESS PLANES: DOODLEBUGS

The doodlebugs were causing much concern, particularly in London. There were clear indications that British defences against them were improving at a great rate, but still many were getting through. In the original Battle for Britain, the enemy bombers had come through in waves, perhaps only once a day. Now, however, the doodlebugs appeared in small groups, with a minimum of warning, any time of the day and night. No one knew when the next bunch would come. So, while the total damage being done was less than previously, they were still very nerve wracking and unsettling.

As you might expect, support for the Brits was again strong.

Letter, Australian. Our British kinsmen are again undergoing a terrible ordeal from the flying-bomb attacks, in what is in effect developing into a second Battle for Britain. Three years ago they won the first Battle for Britain, and in doing so saved the world and civilisation.

We in Australia, who have been spared the bombing ordeals, extend our deepest sympathy to Britain; but I would suggest that we show it in some practical form to help relieve the great distress and suffering which must exist. If the Prime Minister or the Governor-General launched an appeal, I am confident it would meet with a generous response. I will personally subscribe 30 Pounds towards it.

Letter, G Holden. It is possible that in the hearts of many Australians the new suffering of London and the South of England may have superimposed themselves on even our current local events. If such be the case, all we can do is to pray for the sufferers and help the afflicted. In the event of a fund being opened I shall be pleased to contribute 30 Pounds.

Letter, N B. Regarding the proposal to open a fund to help the victims of robot-bombs, could not the churches give their entire collections on some special Sunday, and the racecourses and the picture theatres their takings on a named Saturday?

News item. The Lord Mayor of Sydney said that a few years ago, a fund was created to raise money for the British victims of the Battle for Britain. It was now in recess, but could be revived. He thought that perhaps it could now provide support for Londoners who have become victims of the robot bombs. He was in favour of such a move, and would recommend it to the appropriate Council Committee at their next meeting.

Comment. Events moved faster than the Lord Mayor, and by the time it met, most of the menace had been destroyed.

ANOTHER VIEW OF THE BOMBS

Our propaganda machine, always anxious to spare us worries, kept plying us with the idea that these bombs, although damaging, were not at all technically advanced, and were created by amateur scientists and dithering technicians. The message was that they would not stand the test of time.

One Letter-writer thought differently.

Letters, T Skillman. The current viewpoint of the rocket bomb as a terrorist weapon of little strategic

value argues for a degree of short-sightedness by
the Germans which past history does not bear out.
Why should the Boche – desperately anxious to win
the war – deflect a large part of his technical and
manufacturing effort on to something supposedly
designed to pander only to his vindictiveness and
malevolence? Such a decision could presumably
be taken by a maniacal dictator in a moment of
unbalance, but not by the whole group of ruthless
and undeniably able men who control Germany
today.

No, the robot bomb as reported in the Press is an
uncompleted weapon swung into action before it
was ready, on account of the situation precipitated
by the invasion. In its completed form it will carry
remote control gear and a television eye. It may be
guided almost to its destination by an automatic
pilot, and for the last 30 seconds of its flight
control will be taken over by a mother plane in
the stratosphere carrying duplicate pilot positions.
One pilot in the mother plane will control the bomb
by direct vision; the other will use the television eye
and will receive all the visual and tactile sensations
of sitting in the bomb itself. He will fly it straight
into the target, and will be as hard to stop as the
most accurate pinpoint bombing so far realised by
the Allies.

What defence is there against such a weapon?
Radio interference can do nothing unless the exact
signals used by the enemy are known. How long
will it take to locate these signals, bearing in mind
that they may be on the ether for less than one
minute per bomb? To design the remote control

gear, so that 100 successive bombs could be dispatched without once using the same group of signals, presents little difficulty and demands hardly any complications in the apparatus. Even if some means of finding and jamming the signals is achieved, what will be the result? Simply that the controls will automatically freeze and the bombs will continue on their course. It would never be possible to wrest control from the mother plane and deflect the bomb to explode somewhere harmless.

Why has such a weapon not been developed by the Allies, bearing in mind that no technical difficulties are involved? Or does anyone doubt the technical possibilities? The Army Inventions Board announced recently that such ideas have been before them ever since 1940. Actually a radio controlled dirigible ("being considered by the War Office") was regularly demonstrated on the music halls in 1910. Remote control boats and airplanes were well known long before the present war. The immunity from interference achieved by quite simple devices in regular use in the telephone world is far higher than that needed for the purpose now under discussion.

VICE AND GIRLHOOD

A Sydney doctor, employed by the NSW Health Department, visiting a number of hospitals reported that he was constantly treating young girls for venereal diseases, and that once they were cured, an unfortunately large number went back to prostitution. He called upon the public to take a stance against such happenings, and to make it clear to the girls that such conduct was reprehensible.

There were others who had different approaches.

Letter, M Hickin.   Apparently some relaxation in morals is inevitable in war-time.   Nothing can minimise the gravity, both personally and racially, of sexual promiscuity, but court publicity and the necessity of medical treatment often work a cure. Dr Cooper Booth's revelation of the return to a life of vice by girls previously cured of venereal disease shows that there is not only the expected revolt against tradition and the loss of moral stamina that always accompany abnormal living conditions, but that there is, on the part of some girls, a real abandonment to dissolute living that pays no heed to danger and is quite reckless of consequences.

This is not to be cured by ridicule, as the doctor has suggested.   There must be some lack in the lives of such girls that could be corrected by sound, sympathetic advice, and by constant watchfulness on the part of some disinterested friend.   As a minister's wife, I feel that women gifted with compassion and common sense could handle such cases individually. I am sure there are many who, like myself, would count it a privilege to take a girl under observation after medical treatment and use every effort, by personal contact and frank discussion, to inculcate a sense of responsibility and to re-establish self-respect.

Girls who find it impossible to keep straight should not be ridiculed but helped. The only way to help them is to let them see that there is some one person who is really interested in them as individuals.

Letter, W Coughlan, Christian Social Order Movement, Sydney. As Dr J Booth has recently said, the return of girls to promiscuous sex relations after being cured of venereal diseases with penicillin is melancholy proof of the contention of many Christian people that the discovery and application of quicker and more certain cures of VD would be for many an incitement to sex adventure. This poses a grave dilemma to all concerned – Service and civilian health authorities, social workers, police, parents, the Church, and the community as a whole.

The girls so far detected are of a special type. They are emotionally abnormal, or at best unstable. Whatever may have caused this condition, something must be attempted to deal with the results. The individual treatment suggested by Mrs Hickin is not adequate for this type. Before such offered help can be of much use, the girls need – for their own sake and for the community's – a rude shock. **The hair-shaving treatment** might well be tried here, as it has been in Europe. But it should be followed by a period in a hostel – preferably in the country – where the girls could live healthy and useful lives, have wholesome recreation, and be helped morally and spiritually as well as medically, while their hair grows again. At present the only alternative – gaol – is almost certain to do far more harm than good. Ordinary home life activities, even if the girls would engage in them, would not fill the bill for this type.

If this hostel-in-the-country idea has any merit, could not individuals, organisations, and officials concerned (from various angles) get together and explore the needs and possibilities?

What of the still larger number of girls who drift into promiscuity, but perhaps do not contract disease – or, if they do, are more careful after their first cure? It should by now be clear that the foundations of their delinquency are laid in infancy and childhood; in parental ignorance (not only of sex education, but of ordinary child training), in bad housing, in family discord, in poor recreational facilities, in the prevailing absence of religious and/ or moral conviction, in the fashionable treatment of sex as purely biological, and of human beings as just a special kind of animal, and in the unrealism of so much in the attitude of Christians and of the Church. The remedying of these evils – the continuing evils – is of course a long-term job, requiring the closest co-operation of all relevant agencies. Is there not some step that can be taken at once to make a beginning of such co-operative action?

Letter, Irene Speight. Dr Cooper Booth's statement shows an entire lack of understanding and sympathy in his approach to the problem of the girls cured of VD and returning to the same immoral life.

The problem is social, not medical – penicillin cures the body, but cannot be expected to cure the mind or attitude to life of these girls, many of whom have had little opportunity either of education in its true sense or of decent living conditions.

Surely it is time we realised that society is responsible to a great extent for their control and re-education.

Many of the girls who are dealt with are found to be **sub-normal** and should be treated as such rather than held fully responsible for their actions. To hold them up to ridicule by the suggested method of shaving their heads is a return to barbarism.

GOD'S LITTLE CREATURES

Sydney was crawling with rats. This was also true of the other capital cities. Some people put it down to the shortage of man-power for garbage collection, and for vermin control. Others said that standards of hygiene had deteriorated since the war started. Or maybe it was that rat bait could not be obtained. Or that the housing shortage was promoting living in slums. Whatever the cause, it was indeed lucky that the first writer below had the cure for the problem. Though the second writer casts doubts on this, the spoil-sport.

Letter, A de V MacCallum, Castle Hill. The NES was organised to deal with a Japanese invasion, or air raids. Happily we have been spared these experiences – so far – but another national emergency has arisen out of the war – an invasion of rats.

The NES has an established organisation, an extensive personnel, and gas-masks necessary in fumigating buildings. NES posts could be used as depots for distribution of rat poison and advice.

It has been suggested that such an undertaking would not be popular with NES members. It is difficult to see why a group of patriotic citizens who have voluntarily offered their service for one kind of (possible) war emergency, and have generously given their time to the study and practice necessary to fit them to deal with a potential danger, should not **be equally patriotic** in volunteering for service – less spectacular, but equally, or more, urgent – in a war emergency actually in being. The NES is the obvious body to act, but failing this, could not the Lord Mayor call a public meeting to arrange for organised and concerted action?

Letter, H W Read, NES Warden, Bondi. Referring to the NES and the rat plague, A de V MacCallum said the NES had the "gas masks necessary in fumigating buildings." The gas masks as issued to a warden are useless against the gas used in fumigating, and against ordinary coal gas. This fact is stressed to every warden, and it would be dangerous for anyone to rely upon the gas masks for such work.

TURMOIL IN JAPAN

Two years ago, in mid-1942, the Japanese forces were on top of their part of the world. They had gone as far as they could go, though they did not realise that at the time. From here it was all downhill, with their forces on all fronts gradually being forced back towards Tokyo. As this news gradually sank in, the political forces within Japan that were driving the war had second and third thoughts about what should happen next, and looked for ways to improve the situation.

Over the next few days, the Japanese Prime Minister, General Tojo, resigned. Then the Emperor let it be known that he was unhappy with the war situation and the Cabinet, as a consequence. This, of course, was a good omen for the Allies, and there were hopes that maybe it was a signal that Japan was ready for peace. In the US, the National Convention of the Democrats heard the news in silence, they climbed on their seats, threw their hats in the air, and cheered till they were hoarse. The Vatican also leaked that a Japanese delegation had inferred that the Japs were ready to quit.

The trouble was that the new Japanese Cabinet and hierarchy were once again all drawn from the military, rather than from the civilian ranks of politicians. Quickly, the Press of the nation pronounced that no peace or surrender was on the cards, and that the new leaders were intent on reversing the military losses that had occurred. So, sadly, the war went on, and the troops on the battleground were no better off.

TURMOIL IN GERMANY

If Hitler was now to nominate the worst months of his life, he would have to put July 1944 as right near the top of the list. From a military point of view, no matter where he looked, his forces were suffering terribly.

For example, the Russians were into Latvia, Estonia, almost into Poland and the Americans and the Brits and Canadians were relentlessly moving across Normandy, ever closer to the borders of Germany. In Italy, the Allies were on a slow roll, and in the regions surrounding Turkey, the Russians were grinding forward. The whole of Germany was now **encircled** by massive armies, moving forward with tremendous air support, and showing not one glimmer of mercy.

The only bright light for Hitler was that his doodlebugs, his much-heralded secret weapon, had Londoners scared stiff. But, even there it looked as if that particular menace would soon become ineffectual.

On the morning of July 21st, he and his military chiefs met in a bunker at his headquarters in Wolfchance in Austria. Here, 300 miles from Berlin, in a massive set of concrete bunkers, he attended a noon meeting prior to meeting up with Mussolini in mid-afternoon. An officer, called Staffenberg, arrived at the meeting, with a brief-case with two bombs in it, and placed it on the floor near the feet of seated Hitler.

After a few minutes, the bombs detonated, a few people were killed, but Hitler escaped with torn trousers, a burst eardrum, and soot on his face. He was jubilant for the rest of the day because he considered that he had been spared death by the will of God, and that the episode was a sign of divine approval for his conduct of the war.

In a nation-wide speech at midnight that night he said that the circle of conspirators was extremely small, and that the plot was executed by a tiny band who would be promptly and ruthlessly eliminated, "I was spared a fate which held no horror for me, but would have had terrible consequences for the German people. I see it as a sign from Providence that I must and therefore shall continue my work."

It quickly became apparent that this assassination was **not** the work of a **few** malcontents, but instead was a carefully prepared plot that had been was hatched by senior military officers, and had been months in the making.

In the confusion that followed the explosion, when it was not certain to the German world whether Hitler had survived, the plotters tried to seize military control of Berlin and of Paris. Over a period of a dozen hours, generals and others in those cities arrested each other, troops were called to arms from barracks, a dozen high-ranking officers committed suicide, and a dozen more were executed.

Over the next few weeks, Hitler's vengeful hand extended over the nation. The Staffenberg family was eliminated, the next of kin of other conspirators were arrested and imprisoned, and 5,000 other men and women were executed.

For Hitler himself, the extent of the "treason" was a bitter blow. It came at a time when his failures in the field were growing daily, and he was becoming morose, fitful, and withdrawn. The realisation that such a large number of his officers were prepared to kill him hit him hard, and from here on he became even more isolated and unpredictable.

As I said earlier, July 1944 was a very bad month for Hitler. Then, to top it off, on July 31st, the Americans broke through a strategic Pass at Avranches on the perimeter of France proper, and that left them free to run riot across the plains of France. Paris was within range in the next few weeks.

AUGUST NEWS ITEMS

A number of American entertainers arrived in Sydney to keep the US troops happy in their camps. These included comedian Jack Benny, Carol Landis, and Larry Adler, famous for his mouth-organ skills.

August 3rd. The British Government came clean at last about the damage caused by flying bombs. Prime Minister Churchill said today that **4,735 people had been killed** by them, and 14,000 injured. Also, 17,000 houses had been destroyed, and 800,000 damaged.

Official spokesmen indicated that there could be worse to come. The Germans had started launching a new V2 rocket that would cause even more damage, but very few had hit Britain so far because of technical difficulties. However, it was likely that these would soon be overcome, and **Britain must be ready for heavier bombings**.

August 9th. 6,000 mothers and 11,000 **schoolchildren are leaving London** today in 22 special trains for safe areas.

An Australian lieutenant, who was cashiered from the Army for theft in **1916**, has been proved innocent, and his name has been cleared.

The manufacture of Owen guns at Wollongong in NSW has ceased. The Army says that sufficient stock are now on hand to meet requirements.

From the end of the month, British citizens will be able to send air-mail letters to Australia for sixpence.

New threats to Japan. News item, August 11th. New moves against Japan include a **third Super-Fortress raid** on the Japanese mainland, the first **bombing of the Philippines** since the Japanese invasion, and the shifting of Allied amphibious headquarters to within **1,500 miles of Japan**.

August 16th. **A V2 rocket exploded in the grounds of Buckingham Palace.** It detonated before it hit the ground. It shattered a number of windows, destroyed a summer-house in the grounds, burnt four trees, and ruined a tennis court on which the King was wont to play before the war.

August 21st. **Five boys** were injured when a bakelite hand- grenade exploded. They **were playing with the grenade**, which they had found in bushland near Newcastle.

The Allies were **starting to talk** about **an international body** that would seek to provide world-wide laws after the war. This was along the same lines as the failed League of Nations, that messed up so convincingly after WWI....

The early proposals talked about a group of four nations that would have **veto powers** over decisions made by the body. These powers were USA, UK, Russia and, surprisingly, **China**. These talks led to **the formation of the United Nations**, but China did not get veto powers. In fact it was not admitted at all to the UN until some 30 years later.

JAPANESE POW's AT COWRA

On Saturday August 5th, military authorities announced that a number of Japanese prisoners had escaped from the Cowra camp, in central-southern NSW, at about 2am. They warned local residents that the men were on the loose, and urged them not to give any form of assistance to them. The number of escapees was not specified.

By Monday morning, these authorities proclaimed via the radio, that everyone had been re-captured, and assured people that the menace had gone away.

To almost all Australians, including those in Cowra, this activity seemed like a minor incident, one that was to be expected near a camp of 4,000 Axis prisoners of war. The truth of the matter, was that on that Saturday morning, **545 Japanese escaped from the camp**, and flooded out into the surrounding country-side. Though they were armed with makeshift weapons, but no guns, they were under instructions not to harass civilians in any way, and indeed they did not. They were chased by the soldiers from the camp, and **it took ten days to capture them all.**

Over this time, **231 of them were either killed or committed suicide, and 108 wounded.** Those still living were shipped back to camp.

During the initial break-out, two Aussie soldiers manning a Vickers machine-gun fired into the approaching body of escapes. They were overcome and killed, but not before Private Jones hid the bolt from the gun. This stopped the Japs from turning the gun onto Australian troops. The two heroes, Privates Jones and Hardy, were awarded the George

Cross posthumously as a result of their actions. **A total of four Australians were killed during the incident.**

The camp was maintained as such until the last of the Japs (and Italians) were repatriated in 1947. A Japanese cemetery, and Japanese gardens, were built subsequently at Cowra to honour the Japanese dead.

Comment. The propaganda machine in this nation was in full swing here. The Australian public knew only the very little that was published in the Monday's newspapers and, by then, the attempt had been thwarted, so they were told. It took years for the full story to come out.

Second Comment. A book written by Harry Gordon called *Die Like the Carp*, in 1978, tells the story in detail.

Third Comment. At the time, there were 14,720 Italian prisoners-of-war in Australia, of whom 2,000 were in Cowra. There were also 1,585 Germans, mainly merchant seamen, held at other camps.

TRAINS

Most States had a fairly extensive **electric** train network in their capital cities. In some cases it stretched for about thirty miles in a few directions, and in some cases it was a lot less than this. The carriages were almost universally old and badly sprung, the lighting at night was atrocious, they were always badly cleaned, and there were no automatic doors.

The country trains were all pulled by steam engines, with their white steam and coal-produced black smoke marking their progress. These big beasts, with eight to twelve carriages, set forth into the country areas, on trips of sometimes a thousand miles. Every 100 miles or so they stopped for 10 minutes to take on more water, and for the driver and fireman to have a yarn to whoever was working the water tower.

Each carriage either had a corridor down the centre, or had an aisle down one side of the carriage, and pairs of long seats facing each other reaching to the other side of the train. These were called dog-boxes A constant source of dread to non-drinking travelers was the thought that they might end up seated knee-to-knee with some drunken yobbo, with a bottle of brown musket in a brown paper bag, on a trip of five hundred miles.

The country station-masters were near-relatives of God. They were invited to open small-town shows, flower shows, beauty parades and pet shows. They were often approached for job references, and only mixed with the other town dignitaries, such as the policeman, and local SP bookie and Catholic priest. They made a point of standing at the gate collecting tickets as travelers left the station, and harassed as many schoolboys as possible for not having their three-month term-ticket on them.

Comment. Perhaps by now you have suspected that, in my small coalfields town of Abermain, I did not like the station master.

In any case, this month a number of Letters came in with various grouches against the railways.

Letters, Salt With a Little Savour. Maybe the public will greet with enthusiasm the announcement in your columns that benevolent railway authorities propose **to place cocktail bars on luxury trains** in the post-war millennium. I, a woman of 36, can but tell a simple tale.

In the last four years I have made five over-night train journeys. On two nights on the Melbourne express I had to vacate my seat for the drunken man beside me, and stand seven hours in the corridor. On the third occasion, on the train from Tamworth, the affair was mild – there was only abusive, savoury breath on the hourly intrusion of the military police and ticket collectors. On the fourth, from Singleton, the fellow was helplessly restless, and kept the compartment in a tension not reduced when he bought two bottles of oysters and drank each at a draught. Still, he carried his oysters like a gentleman. On the fifth my sole compartment companion was torpid, so I stretched out and slept.

Of course, having undergone some eight years' university education, and being now entitled to two-thirds the income of a charwoman, I travel second class. Some day I may be able to change my occupation, and join the plutocrats who can afford a week's rest from labour to consider the actions of the local butcher, and then, perhaps, I shall be able to travel first class, and know how the **genteel** inebriate behave.

Maybe, the benevolent designers of luxury trains have not failed to consider the problems suggested above, and have planned luxury topers' compartments (all futurist cons), and free medical and pharmaceutical services for the period of transit. But designers are artists. They know the value of suspense. No doubt we shall hear all about that when the millennium comes. In the meantime, we have our waking dreams.

The railway authorities, I have no doubt are serving the interests of the people. Which people?

Letters, M M. The Railway Department complains of "scalers" on the trains, and some time ago put the public to much inconvenience with the banning of platform tickets. This was my experience travelling from the north coast:

I bought a first-class ticket, and later the compartment became crowded with travelers. An inspector boarded the train in the Newcastle area, and on inspection found five people in the compartment travelling on second-class tickets. Not only were these people not asked to pay the difference in fare, but nothing whatever was said to them about their dishonesty. If the department intends that no action be taken for this sort of thing then it is time it made all travelling in the State one class.

Letters, Travel By Train. As a regular interstate traveler to Brisbane by the Limited express, I feel that I am expressing the opinion of passengers when I state that the New South Wales railway authorities should not waste time dreaming of post-war luxury in travel, but instead, should realise that the comfort of passengers on this journey is now sadly overlooked.

The by-law banning smoking in non-smoking compartments should be strictly enforced; the placing of "frozen" foot-warmers in the train at Sydney is absurd; the inadequate and obnoxious lavatory facilities should be improved; the practice of the conductor on the Sydney Limited from Brisbane of informing passengers nine hours after the departure of this train that sleeping berths "are now available," is ridiculous, when these could have been booked at Brisbane prior to journey; Coff's Harbour refreshment room should cater for a hot, substantial meal for travelers on this 19 hours' trip.

The proposal of cocktail bars on trains is to be deplored, in view of many past complaints of annoyance to travelers through unseemly conduct, as a result of alcohol.

Letters, J Sexton. With horrible frequency we read of people being killed or injured by falling from electric trains through the open doors. A simple technical device for the automatic closing of doors on moving trains would prevent this, and should have been introduced long ago.

THE REFERENDUM

Voting was on Saturday, August 21ˢᵗ. By then, the political Parties had presented their arguments over and over, and everyone was sick of it. **Labour** basically said that the country had emerged from the threat of invasion because the Government had given itself almost dictatorial powers, and this meant the restrictions on some liberties for the individual. It had set up Departments and bureaucracies that had necessarily been tough on the average citizen, and had pushed around and conscripted many people against

schemes as those outlined in the article "Building a New Darwin." In no case has any notice been taken of the opinions of Darwin residents. They have to live in the Government-planned town but their experience and practical knowledge of the necessities of the place are always disregarded.

Shortly before the Japanese bombers came over, the Government announced that Darwin was to become a garden city, apparently overnight, and they began planting flowering shrubs and trees along some of the streets. But no effort was made to put the Darwin streets in good order first, so the effect resembled a man wearing a clean collar who had forgotten to wash his neck.

There were streets, in the centre of the town, where folk had to walk in the roadways, because there were no footpaths provided. In some streets, motor cars travelled along the footpaths because there was no roadway, just rocky gullies. The Esplanade, which could have been made a wonderful driveway, was so narrow in parts that two cars could pass only with difficulty, and it had sharp turns in most inconvenient places.

Residents pointed out these anomalies to the Government, only to be told that we did not appreciate all the advantages which were being bestowed upon us, and that we were most ungrateful people.

Have the architects who are planning a new Darwin considered these matters, or will they ignore the experiences of those who have worked and planned for a new Darwin?

In Darwin we prefer two-storey residences. The upstairs rooms are cool at night, and are used as bedrooms; and the downstairs premises are cool all day, and there we work. We want verandahs, 12 feet to 18 feet wide, for on these we entertain our friends, eat, and often sleep. As we wear whites or light clothing, which needs frequent laundering, we want ample water and full facilities for laundries.

Letter, H Rowe. I am concerned with suggestions that when the armistice with Germany is announced, the nation should rejoice and take the rest of the day off work. There are also suggestions that the next day should be a public holiday.

This is absurd in Australia. We will still be engaged in a full-time war in the Pacific, with a Japanese enemy that will still be producing flat out while we have our day of celebrations and, doubtless, debauchery.

Will our 20,000 prisoners-of-war be allowed out for the period? Will their anxious families be given a period where they can stop worrying about them? What we should do is for everyone to work a few hours longer, inspired by the thought that the harder and longer we work, the sooner **our** war will be over.

Comment. A few days later, John Curtin made a statement that made the same points that Mr Rowe had made. It was to be official policy. There was to be no relaxation at the time of the European armistice. But who knows. Not everyone thought that there would be a European armistice. In an interview from the German Foreign Office, Hitler said:

"No longer can military standards alone be applied in gauging the prospects of victory. Those who previously declared that the war was lost for Britain when France went down or that the Soviet was inevitably doomed when the Ukraine and the Donets Basin were invaded now know better – to their own cost.

"Those who at present believe that Germany is lost when the enemy stands on the Rhine are guilty of the same error. Our military reverses of past months have been clearly traced to their sources and taken to heart. Germany must conquer because otherwise the Reich will go under. **Germany can conquer and Germany will conquer.**"

THE BUNDY CLOCK

Here was a new invention, fresh from the land of the Stars and Stripes. In case you have long forgotten its purpose, let me remind you that it was a clock, placed near the entrance to a factory. When the employees entered or left the premises, they thrust their cards into the clock and their times were recorded on the card. This provided pay-roll data, but also a clear-cut, precise record of the comings, and goings, of employees.

Australian workers were not at all keen on these new methods of controlling them. Below, however, is one worker who saw their value.

Letter, A Crowther. Mr Harold Meggitt's statement that the bundy clock was "a machine of the devil instituted to show men they are serfs," is not substantiated by general experience. Objection is taken to the bundy clock, as to other practices operating for the orderly conduct of business through discipline, by the inveterate late-comers and others among employees who hold the culpable view that it is not unmoral to beat the boss for time – the time for which the boss pays.

But those usually are minority sections. Employees in the majority display a finer sense of obligation to their employers, a greater spirit of loyalty to their jobs. And who among workers enjoying such wages and conditions as apply in Australia would consider himself or herself demeaned by conforming to a fair and accurate method of timekeeping?

THE LAW IS THE LAW

The Second Victory Loan was opened in Oz to raise money to help pay for the war. The authorities always opened the loan with a big bang ceremony. As part of it, they planned to sound all the sirens on Sydney Harbour for a few minutes. However, the Maritime Services Board advised that this was not possible because of **war-time regulations**. It would not listen to arguments that said there was now no danger in sounding off.

LABOUR SUPPORTS SOCIALISM STILL

The **Commonwealth Housing Commission** has sent a recommendation to Government for **the nationalisation of all land in Australia**. "This is a new twist to the cause of socialism, and will doubtless be opposed by any person who holds land." **Forget it: it won't happen**, but it shows the desire of some bodies for greater control of activities by the Labour Party.

OCTOBER NEWS ITEMS

More crockery, cutlery, and domestic cooking utensils will soon be available for sale in Australia.

The Prime Minister, John Curtin on October 1st completed **nine years as leader of the Federal Labour Party**. This is a **record** term in office.

In early October, **share prices** listed on the public Exchanges were all subject to a **maximum price level**. That meant that even if you were prepared to pay more than the level, it was not possible to do so. **Each share had its own level**, based on history. Now, **the level was to be raised** by 10 per cent, or ten shillings, whichever was the smallest.

A lady running a boarding house in Sydney's Redfern found some powders in her letter-box. She took them to the police, and they found that strychnine had been mixed with the normal **headache powder**.

The above news is of little consequence to us, except to remind us of the **two brands that dominated the very large headache-powder market in Oz**. One was **APC**. The other was **BEX**. Does anyone else recall them? Perhaps if I say that you should "**have a cup of tea, a Bex, and a good lie down**" you will remember them.

Teachers in the armed services who were not fit for active duty, and **who were over 35, would now be released.**

On October 9th, newspaper readers in Sydney were surprised on waking to find that their **daily newspapers were reduced in size to four pages,** and it came from the **combined efforts of the four dailies**. That is, from the *SMH*, the *Daily Telegraph*, and the evening papers the *Sun* and the *Daily Mirror*.

Journalists at these papers had gone on **an indefinite strike**, claiming more wages and better conditions. Management staff at the papers were able to produce the four page composite edition. **Doubtless, more will be heard of this**.

October 21st. News item. The newspapers are again allowed to **publish weather reports.** They ceased publication of these **three years ago** because it was thought that the Japs might use them to their advantage. There were many people who thought that **yesterday's** report would be of no use to the enemy, but the Government argued that the weather comes in sequences, and that yesterday's weather could be used to forecast the future. In any case, **residents got their first forecast in three years.** Someone wrote in and said that it hadn't changed much.

The war at sea continues. News item October 27th. **HMAS Australia** was damaged **superficially** during the invasion of the Philippines. **Nineteen officers and crew, including the Commanding Officer, Captain Dechaineux, were killed.** The war was still taking its terrible toll of servicemen and their families.

Was Dobell's portrait of Joshua Smith really a portrait? We should find out soon, because in Sydney, on the 24th of this month, a Court case to decide this got underway. Dobell was there, and so too was Joshua Smith.

WOULD YOU LIKE A DRINK?

The Oz community had plenty of money, due to steady work and lots of overtime. So, sections of it were quite happy to regale themselves with a drink or two. Or perhaps three. The problem with this was that it was hard to get a steady supply of grog. And it was hard to find a decent place to drink it in.

Every reader of this book will be familiar with the images of the six-o'clock swill, with big men crammed into small bars jostling for beer at the end of the day. But they were sometimes the lucky ones, because pubs were often shut for much of the day, or for a whole week-end. In any case, beer was likely to run out at any time, "the keg's gone", leaving a horde of drinkers wondering where they could find a watering hole where the beer was "on".

This was **the official version**. If you want **reality** you have to add the illegal after-hours drinking in every pub, the availability of scarce bottled beer for select customers with a quid to spare, the occasional bottle of whisky or spirits for those with two quids to spare, and the regular supply of bottles of methylated spirits and plonk for thirsty Aborigines.

In restaurants, the situation was no better. Wine was almost unheard of, though brown musket or sherry might be sold in high-class joints. Whisky was on sale at enormous prices, but only it seemed to racketeers. In short, the liquor business was in glorious chaos, with plenty of profits for the black-marketers, and random scraps for the serious drinkers in the general population.

It was hardly surprising then that at times politicians and others would start a push for liquor reform. Actually, politicians generally solemnly cried out for changes to the laws and venues, but then sadly intoned that, "due to the war" it was not **now** the right time to do it. Many churches also campaigned steadily for changes, but they meant that grog should be banned altogether. The general population, though, knew full well that reform was not at all likely, and satisfied itself with that wonderful feeling of having a justified non-stop grizzle about the situation.

Having said that, I must point out that occasionally the issue flared up in the newspapers. Below are a few Letters from the latest blaze.

Letters, North Shore. Some years ago I spent a month in Stockholm and returned full of praise for the "Bratt" system in vogue there. There is so much merit in this system that Australia should seriously consider its introduction in this country.

The basic principle of the system is individual control of all sales, the selling agency must know the identity of the buyer, and keep track of the quantity of liquor sold and the date of sale. A customer, therefore must always make **his purchases at the same retail shop**, where **a complete card-register is kept of all clients**. Persons who have been found guilty of the misuse of alcohol, illegal traffic in liquor, or of similar misdemeanours, are temporarily or permanently deprived of their right to purchase at all. **On registration, clients receive a pass-book, and all sales are entered in it.** Wine may be bought in unlimited quantities, but no one can obtain more than a maximum of four litres of **spirituous** liquor a month. Only about 30 per cent of all pass-book owners, however, are entitled to a ration of four litres. The big majority receive considerably less. At restaurants, guests are served a maximum of 15 centi-litres, and only in conjunction with the taking of the meal. The manufacture and sale of wines and spirits are supervised by the State through a board of control, while all import and wholesale business is in the hands of a semi-official institution.

Letters, Panamite.   The Australian climate is ideally suited to the open-air café restaurant – more so, indeed, than that of Paris, home of the "café de terrace." But Australians prefer to gobble in the congested corridors of cafes and guzzle in gloomy, gaol-like "pubs." If a person were seen being served with a drink anywhere than between four walls, a shocked crowd would stare, and there would be an outcry. Any good drink takes on an added sparkle and colour, tastes better, does you a power of good in the sunlight.

Letters, Walter Burke.   Sydney and Paris are not comparable in their inhabitants or as cities, from the point of view of location or surroundings. We must face the fact that **Sydney is a windy and grimy city, and this cannot be remedied**. It is largely due to the fact that Sydney is splendidly tempered by the north-easters coming up practically every afternoon, these winds are so strong as to make eating and drinking out-of-doors exceedingly uncomfortable.

Again, the Parisian temperament is entirely different; light wines, not beer or spirits, are the usual drink. There is practically no drunkenness. Moreover, normally, all work ceases for two hours in the middle of the day, and over a café crème or a glass of wine many business transactions are discussed and finalised in these places.

There is another point: Paris has very wide streets, and the municipal authorities are willing to lease the areas for footpath restaurants and, to meet such a demand, Sydney's streets would have to be standardised to about 90 feet wide – at least. Many of the above comments apply to most other Continental cities with which I am familiar.

Letters, Traveller. Surely all the world knows that Australia, with her climate, needs, above all things, the open air café restaurant of all European continental countries.   Many thousands of our citizens have seen them at work in many cities in Europe. More thousands of our returned troops of the last war have seen them in countless estaminets in France and Belgium. And yet for a quarter of a century we have stood for the uncivilised 6pm closing, with all that it entails of illegal after-hours trading is every country town and the daily rush guzzling between 5 and 6pm in every city bar.

Licensing reform came in England after the last war, and as a result drunkenness has practically ceased to exist.

The essence of the matter is food and sociable drinking, unhurried and at tables. In Britain, food is compulsorily married to every pub – not free counter lunches, but food for sale in every type of bar at all opening hours. Here, food is divorced from drinking. Restaurants cannot sell drinks; pubs do not sell food. Is it not Gilbertian?

ATTITUDE TO MODERN ART

Letters, Tom Darcy. Modern art needs to be brought before the public in a comprehensible, intelligent manner by those who know art. At the moment this portrayal is being usurped by the inane criticism of people who expect a likeness of photographs at an exhibition. The latter intolerant prejudice is having a pernicious influence on public appreciation, which could destroy any hope of the general acceptance of modern art.

Letter, V J Dowling. The Australian public's intolerant objection to modern art is hardly creditable. There seems very little hope for art in this country if the people continue to throw up hands of horror and amazement at an innovation that they do not understand.

A similar attitude was adopted to Impressionism when the movement was first introduced, but once understood the art was acknowledged and now such names as Van Gogh, Gauguin, Cezanne, and Degas rank equally among the great masters of the older schools of pure art. Impressionism should have accustomed people to innovation no matter how radical.

Admittedly, no matter what type they were, very few examples of modern art in Sydney at the moment could be called good art, but this is the only justifiable criticism. It is grossly unfair to contemporary artists to have their work condemned incomprehensibly by people with no knowledge of art as a subject. It is also damning to have the narrow, perverted opinion of officialdom publicised simply because it reads some obscene meaning, of which the artist is unaware, into a good painting.

STRIKES GALORE

Every one was sick of war-time regulations. Every one was sick and tired of all sorts of people hiding behind the war to foist restrictions and prohibitions on them. People wanted someone to say officially that the nation could relax a lot, that victory was in sight, and that there would be a more relaxed world round the corner.

In workplaces all over the nation, there were workers who were taking stock of where they were. They looked at how hard they had been working, for years, and they looked at their work conditions, and at their pay. They could see that in Britain, the workers were now fighting great industrial battles for more improvements, and were slowly getting them. It was dawning on them that the time had come to better their own lot. To hell with the idea of patriotic work-till-you-drop, to hell with the idea that we were still under a war-time threat. What the workers wanted was more wages, more holidays, better and safer work conditions, and with that came the realisation that the only way to get these thing was to strike.

So October saw a huge increase in the number and intensity of strikes in the entire nation. It was as if someone had pressed a "strike button", and this had turned the whole population from working into striking.

THE NEWSPAPER STRIKE.

This was the grand-daddy of them all. On Monday the 9th of October, newspaper readers across NSW sat down with their Weet Bix, opened up the paper, and found only four pages. Some of them looked at the mast head, and found that the paper came from a combination of the *Herald, Telegraph, Sun and Mirror.* There was clearly something wrong here, because these four Sydney dailies were normally scarcely on speaking terms.

It turned out that earlier, members of the Printers and Kindred Industry Union (PKIU) had presented a log of claims for improvements, and this had been rejected. On Saturday morning, a bunch of them had called a strike, and by Sunday it had spread to the other three dailies, and also to the many other unions in the newspaper industry. So papers stopped being printed.

The newspaper proprietors reacted by deciding to print their own four-page edition daily, and it was this that readers got on the Monday morning. For the next ten days this was repeated daily, until the dispute was settled by arbitration, and the strikers went back to work. There were quite a few delicious asides to all this.

First. For the owners. The decision by the newspaper proprietors to issue a combined paper was against the law. The Federal Minister for Customs pointed out that war-time regulations **prohibited the publication of any newspaper that had not been approved by the Government**. To get this approval would take months, so the barons went ahead anyway. They were not subsequently prosecuted.

Second. For the strikers. The NSW government, strongly influenced by the Labour Party, got involved. It obviously supported the strikers, so it allowed Railways **to ban the carriage of the reduced paper to country areas**, and to Sydney suburbs. Later, the newspapers sued the Railways for this, but it never came to court.

Third. For the strikers. Every day, the normal thing was for newspapers to begin their trips to the reader by being dumped on the footpath outside the local paper-shop, and then they were wrapped by the newsagent and delivered. But, this system was disrupted by unionists **who got up earlier than the agents, and stole and destroyed the four-page spread**, and left the householder with nothing to read.

Fourth. For the strikers. Some readers will remember the **paper-boys** who used to mill round railway stations, and bus and tram stops, selling papers to gathering pedestrians. These young men got into the action as well, and refused to sell papers during the strike.

Fifth. The arbitration system got a bit of a shake up. There were too many jurisdictions, too many tribunals, too many courts, far too many unions, that all had a say in setting awards and conditions. Nothing specific came out of this strike in this regard, but it was made perfectly clear, again, that the **arbitration system was a mess** and something had to be done about it. In fact, something material **was** done, **after a few decades.**

Six. The *Sydney Morning Herald* dropped its pretence of impartiality, and gave **a superb display of one-sided**

reporting. Normally, you could expect that paper to give a reasonably balanced coverage of news. Granted it was a paper run by capitalists and it was committed to present the capitalist viewpoint. Thus, it was certain that it could never find any merit in the actions of **any** strikers, and it laid the boot into the miners particularly. Still, it did it in a distant way, with a conservative and **somewhat** balanced approach.

This was not the case in **this strike that affected itself**. It came out with all guns ablaze, and used every limited column-inch to bore it up the strikers. For example, it scarcely mentioned that the creation of a composite newspaper was breaking the law. And, as another example, it used up several of its valuable column-inches to publish Letters like the following.

Letters, J Maclean. Despite the disability under which we are placed through lack of the usual daily newspapers, I trust that you will not yield to illegal force. The spirit of blackmail levied in the community by bodies trying to obtain benefits to which the law does not entitle them, and the fostering of this spirit by professional party politicians, is breeding a general contempt of law and order and civic responsibility.

Letters, A Mosman. Whatever the original rights or wrongs of the dispute between Associated Newspapers and the printing industry may be, a very sinister note has now crept into the whole proceedings.

It now appears obvious that it is a well-organised plot to disorganise the press and thus provide certain members of the Government with the opportunity of using this dislocation of public service as a means to gain even greater control over the freedom of the people.

Letters, Silurian.   The newspaper proprietors are to be congratulated on the firm stand they are taking against the strikers now checking the issue of news in this city. If there is not something underneath it is difficult to understand how this unscrupulous militant minority of the union could have overruled the majority in a matter of principle.

Comment. These limp little pieces hardly present a second or third side to the argument.

THE END OF THE STRIKE

On the Friday of the second week of the strike, it was declared to be over. Over the last twelve days, the goodies and baddies, and politicians from all sides, had traded insults, and legal arguments, and pressure tactics, left, right and centre. The courts and tribunals and commissions had been filled with applications, writs, injunctions, and dozens of lawyers and barristers and judges, most of them working to settle the strike, and a few of them not at all interested in doing this. In short, it was **a normal big strike, and it went through the normal processes.**

The settlement was a fizzer. Issued under the Commonwealth Industrial Commission, it stipulated that all workers who had been sacked during the strike should be re-instated, and then not victimised when back on the job. It pointed out that it could not grant extra leave, or money, or a shorter working week, because these were **all**

fixed by war-time regulations, and could be varied only in exceptional circumstances. It gave the PKIU **permission to argue** that special circumstances did in fact apply, and that a hearing would be held at a later date.

Comment. The spokesman for the barons said that "the result achieved by the strike is exactly nil", and he was pretty close to the truth. The one advance for the strikers was to **gain the chance to argue their case at a later date**, and they did not have that chance before the strike.

OTHER STRIKES

While this was going on, workers were walking off the job all over the place. For example, NSW butchers provided half the normal supply of meat for a few days, then provided none for a full week, and then half supplies for another two days. NSW Public Transport workers stopped working the trains and buses for a one-day stoppage. All over the nation, not just NSW, employees downed tools, and said they would stop work for a day or a week or more.

Their claims were the familiar ones. They wanted more money, more holidays, shorter working hours, and safer and better conditions. Their employers said they could not be granted because of war-time restrictions, and anyway they could not afford them.

There were plenty of Letters once the newspapers got back to their normal size.

Letters, T J Ryan. Industrial laws, without which there can be no industrial or civil order, are being contemptuously swept aside, and mob rule makes its uncontrolled will the only guide as to what conditions shall prevail in industry. Whether the people are deprived of their usual food supplies or light or fuel or newspapers is of no more consequence than the violation of the industrial laws.

When Governments that are responsible for the observance of the laws remain passive while the laws are thus violently ignored, such passiveness must be regarded only as evidence of their unfitness to govern.

Letters, S G, Mosman. How much longer is a suffering public going to tolerate the anarchic conditions existing today? The worst aspect is the contempt with which the law is treated and the utter failure of a State and Federal Government to enforce it.

If the State or the Federal Government cannot administer the law and do it impartially, it is time for it to get out and let a more resolute Government replace it. Public protests and mass meetings by housewives would assist to remind the Government that decent Australians have been bullied quite enough while they are strenuously engaged fighting a war to bring peace, security, and freedom to the world.

Letters, A Hebblewhite. People, particularly in New South Wales, must rise above sectionalism and selfish ends if we expect to retain the respect of our Allies and a post-war economy other than slavery. Russia, the country so admired by extremist agitators, went through the same trials and tribulations as we are now experiencing and found that social welching could not be permitted in any circumstances without facing economic ruin. **Industrial malcontents find themselves with a firing squad** and a brick wall when interfering with the war effort and asking for more than their share in a Soviet economy. Because the people are apathetic and do not understand, we have made no combined protest, and **a people's union** with a few simple public-spirited objectives is the only medium through which it can be done.

Letters, A. C. A. D A S C has struck a significant note concerning the "sickness" of the community. The general acceptance of these "social phenomena", which are undermining our morale, is a definite indication of a spiritual deterioration which threatens our whole social structure.

There is a general attitude in the community of "What's in it for me?" and an abuse of freedom which our leaders are doing nothing to check. Rather do they encourage it by spineless toleration, either deliberately or by reason of force majeure exercised by their political bosses – a lamentable state of affairs which can only end in chaos.

Comparatively speaking, we in Australia (with the exception of those who have given their dear ones) do not know there is a war on. As for privation, we don't know what it means. We are full fed, unfettered and self-indulgent to a degree which must be nauseating to our own brave boys, and especially to our kinsfolk in the Mother Country, but for whose heroic endurance of suffering and hardship we would most assuredly have been sunk in the depths of serfdom long ago. They are now sending their war-weary troops over here to assist us further in the preservation of this precious freedom of ours, which, by selfishness and cupidity we are unconsciously but surely frittering away.

To quote a distinguished Englishman after the last war: "Unless we can produce an adequate number of men and women who will put God first, their country second, their class third, and themselves last, we shall lose our liberties, and we shall deserve to lose them."

Comment. The views expressed here by these serious-minded people are solemn and strong. They reflect a view in society at large that strikers had gone too far, and that the strike weapon should be moderated. But **how** changes to awards and conditions could be achieved, **given the war-time restrictions**, remained unanswered by anyone.

OZ's OWN CAR

Various government agencies were discussing **setting up an Australian car industry after the war.** Approaches have been made to Ford, General Motors Holden, Chrysler-Dodge, and **the Australian firm, Die Casters Ltd**. It was thought that at least 20,000 cars would need to be produced to become viable.

Comment. Rubbish talk. It will never happen.

NOVEMBER NEWS ITEMS

The 700th Beaufort bomber **built in Australia** went into service with the RAAF on November 1st.

Only **13 out of every hundred houses** surveyed by the Sydney City Council in slum pockets of the city conformed, or could be made to conform, to **minimum health standards**. It was said that the same conditions applied in similar pockets in **all cities** round the nation.

Heavier penalties would be imposed for failure to lodge **gift duty** returns.

Over one million acres of wheat in NSW, and also half the oats crop, **have failed completely due to the drought.** People are saying that it is being **caused by long-term climate change.**

It was alleged in Sydney's Central Court yesterday that a man and his wife, owners of a rest home for the elderly, **had forged the wills of three occupants.**

The existing President, **Roosevelt, was re-elected** in the USA. This will be his fourth term in office, and this is a record. Legislation passed soon after **limited the presidential terms to two only.** That is, a total of eight years.

More **corsets** will become available soon, and this will relieve **the acute shortage** a little. Authorities say that more materials have reached the country, and that workers will be allocated to do the manufacturing.

A vast pall of dust from the parched inland enveloped the whole of **eastern Australia** yesterday. Hot depressing conditions brought home to city dwellers **the seriousness of the drought.**

A paratrooper in the US Army, was **hanged in Brisbane for the murder** of Doris Roberts on June 18th.

November 15, News item. Sunday's daring raid on Tromso Fiord **sank Germany's last battleship, Tirpitz,** with the loss of 700 crew.

News item. "**Palestinian terrorism.** Mr Churchill in a statement denounced Jewish terrorism in Palestine." Without taking sides in the matter, I remind readers that **conflict in Israel and Palestine is not a recent event.**

The Acting Prime Minister, Frank Forde, announced today that in September **a Japanese ship**, carrying 700 Australian and 500 British troops, **had been torpedoed by US submarines**, and that about **950 men had died**. Obviously the subs were **not aware** that the POWs were on the ship.

Two days later Mr Forde announced in Parliament that in June another ship **carrying Australian POWs** had similarly been sunk, and **184 men had died**.

Because householders are **hoarding biscuit tins**, the manufacture of biscuits in Oz is being curtailed.

The **first Aborigine to reach Officer rank** in the army has been commissioned recently.

WHAT MAKES A PORTRAIT?

Remember that earlier artist William Dobell entered a painting of a gentleman called Joshua Smith into the prestigious Archibald Prize competition? Remember too that there were claims that the painting was a caricature, and not a portrait, and so was not eligible to be entered, and so he could not get the Prize. At last the matter came to the Equity Court, with the NSW Attorney General acting on information from persons Joseph Wolinski and Mary Edwards.

Over a week was taken up with proceedings. It was described as a battle between connoisseurs, and between experts, and it all centred on what was the definition of a portrait. It was marked by juicy testimony and opinions from many of the nation's artists and promoters, all of whom had their own personal idea of what a portrait should achieve. The court was persistently crowded, and "some of those who were able to find seating were wont to exclaim or applaud as the various statements of experts were cast before them."

On the fourth court day, Dobell was in the box. Here is a small except.

Dobell: "I painted Joshua Smith as he appears to me, and with the licence that I can claim as an artist."

Barrister, Mr Barwick: You could have conveyed the same information without resorting to these devices? – Not of the real Joshua Smith. At one particular moment I could have done it objectively, but not the Joshua Smith I knew.

Do you call that picture a representation of his appearance? – I would say 90 per cent.

Is that his mouth? – I am glad you mentioned that. It was the only thing the model criticised.

Just answer the question. – The answer is "Yes."

What about the shape of the head, the nose, the neck? – Yes all 90 per cent. But I might as well criticise your conduct of the case by calling attention to your wig as to take the picture piece by piece. The whole thing seems to me an obvious good likeness.

You set out to create first a picture? – A portrait and a picture.

It was not painted originally for the exhibition? – Yes, it was.

Was there not a period when it was designed for some other purpose? – I do not remember anything like that. I think that entry in the competition was the sole purpose.

I mean the inception of it? – I cannot say.

It had its inception in a jest? – I do not paint in jest.

That is not what I ask. Will you deny that the inception of this painting was in a jest? – I do deny that.

And that its entry in the competition was a great uncertainty until a late stage? – I would not say that.

You would not deny it? – No.

Did you make any attempt to put faithfully on canvas what you saw when you looked at Joshua Smith? – Of course I did.

Do you tell us this is in the tradition of Rembrandt? – I like to think so.

You regard Rembrandt as a master who would record with the degree of exaggeration that is present in this picture? – I think he would if it accorded with the getting of the character of the person he was trying to portray.

As Joshua Smith sat before you, did he physically appear to your eyes, at any time as he appears now on that canvas? – Yes, within those limits that I have mentioned. On an artistic point you can't answer yes or no.

Leave art out of it. – But you can't leave art out of it.

When Mr Barwick repeated the question on physical appearance, Mr Dwyer (for Dobell) objected, and Mr Justice Roper said: "You must attribute to your client a degree of intelligence which he appears to be exhibiting."

Applause from the back of the court-room at this remark brought a quick shout of "Silence" from the court orderly.

On the subject of physical proportions in portrait-painting, Mr Dobell said: "You could take 95 per cent of the pictures entered for the Archibald Prize, and I guarantee not 10 per cent show the precise proportions."

Mr Barwick: That may be because of their deficiencies. – Wouldn't you allow me a deficiency?

In the design of the picture, what part do the red handkerchief and tie take? – He happened to be wearing a red handkerchief, and I thought it was a good colour note. I have seen him wearing a red tie and a red cardigan.

So it went on. Early in November, the decision was handed down. Justice William Roper gave the opinion that despite the startling exaggeration and distortion that was clearly intended by the artist, the painting was undoubtedly a pictorial representation of the subject, and he found that it was a portrait within the meaning of John Archibald's will. He said that he was not called upon to decide whether the painting was good or bad. He found that the challenge was dismissed, and awarded costs against the two artists who brought the application.

Comment. Joshua Smith was a talented artist, and himself won the Archibald Prize in 1944. He described Dobell's painting as "a curse, a phantom that haunts me. It has torn at me every day of my life. I've tried to bury it inside me in the hope that it would die. But it never does."

Dobell was considerably disturbed by the court action, and moved away from city life to the shores of Lake Macquarie, where he spent years painting landscapes, though he did do a famous collection of portraits a few years later

Was the matter settled? On the one hand, a Mr John Young, recently Acting Director of the National Art Gallery, said that "the issue is not settled. The question that the Court has not answered is whether eccentricity, formlessness and ugliness are to supplant rationality, form, and truth in the art of the future."

On the other hand, the current Acting Director said that the soundness of the judgment permitted no further adverse judgment. **The art world appeared about as unified as normal**.

TAKEN FOR A RIDE BY MANPOWER

It is timely to remind you that Manpower had not gone away. Let me illustrate this by reference to its involvement with a jockey John Duncan, who lived in Sydney, and who had **applied for permission to travel to Melbourne to ride in the Melbourne Cup**. Four other Sydney jockeys, Darby Monroe, George Podmore, Neville McGrowdie, and Billie Cook, had applied successfully.

It might have been expected that there would be no problem. But Manpower had a long memory. It turns out that Duncan had been sent by them to work in a wire factory, on the 3 pm to mid-night shift. He then had to get up at 3 am to start his track-work. He weighed well under seven stone, and heavy work in the factory and the long day there and on the track took their toll, and his work attendances suffered. Then three months ago, he was moved to day work, his health improved, so his work record was now good. He pointed out that he had twice been rejected by the army, and was rejected because of his size. But that meant he was no "slacker."

Manpower, however, remembered his diminished attendance, and so now refused him permission to ride, in the Melbourne Cup. **The Melbourne Cup, mind you.**

Comment. We should even now be ever-thankful to Manpower for their efforts in thus keeping Australia free from the dreaded Japs.

THE FORTUNES OF JOHN CURTIN

Curtin had been weathering the war well, **politically**. Up till now, he had kept his small majority in Parliament, and had survived the juvenile actions of a few of his ratbag Ministers. Importantly, though, he had kept the respect and, in some cases, the devotion, of most people. They admired his straight talking, his undoubted hard work, and his determination to serve Australia's interests.

Now, however, a few doubts were showing up about his performance. In particular, he was being attacked because he was doing nothing to stop the strikes. As I have mentioned earlier, the trouble for him here was that the Labour Party had its base firmly fixed in the unions, and there was no way he could attack the unions by opposing strikes. So all he could do really was sound off against them, but what he could actually achieve was exactly nothing.

So that is what he did. This attracted criticism, and it was becoming a bit more personal.

Letters, W Shelley. During these past years of anxiety and strain it would not seem unreasonable to expect the Prime Minister of Australia to have gone among the people and given sympathy and encouragement to all who have so loyally given of their best for the nation.

Has there been any occasion when Mr Curtin has moved among the people or visited members of our fighting forces at battle stations or elsewhere? He has spoken from a microphone at Canberra in support of war loans, and in the town halls of capital cities, but one would expect something more outstanding from a Prime Minister. Notwithstanding Mr Churchill's onerous duties he has repeatedly found time to appear in person and to offer cheer and encouragement to the civilian population of England as well as to his fighting men in the field.

Why does this great gulf between Mr Curtin and people exist? Why must he remain Leader of the Labour Party all the time but Prime Minister for only some of it, instead of the other way about?

Then there was this Letter, not aimed at Curtin only, but capturing the general mood of the public. People were tired of the endless exhortations, from Curtin especially, that urged them to tighten their belt, and save, and basically worry a lot and be miserable.

Letters, Joan Wilkinson. I quote below from a recent letter from my husband, a sergeant now in his fourth year of service in the AIF, who is somewhere in the South-west Pacific area.

Today being 11th November, Armistice Day, I suppose Sydney will stand reverently silent for two minutes and then rush madly back to making fortunes out of a later and a better war. That brings me to the point of morale. The Allied Governments are playing a very dangerous game with their repeated warnings of a "long, hard struggle ahead," etc., etc. **That is one of the worst things they can tell a soldier. He gets a hopeless feeling about it all**. As for the civilians, if they are doing their bit, it affects them in the same way, whereas it encourages the black marketeers and profiteers to launch out into bigger and better enterprises.

Why the hell can't the Allies work on the other track – "One more terrific punch and war will be over" – or words to that effect. I believe they can and will end it fairly quickly, so why not tell the truth and try to inspire everyone into a final short, tremendous effort? Or are they deliberately prolonging things? I wonder."

News Items. November 6th. It was revealed yesterday that Prime Minister Curtin had been placed in hospital **for a few days.** It was stated that he needed a complete rest from his arduous duties.

November 8th. John Curtin has been kept in hospital, and it has been determined that, due his **being so run down**, he will be away from his work **for some weeks**.

November 11th. The medical report on Curtin refers to some strain on his heart, and that will require **two months of rest**.

Comment. There could be no doubt that, as a correspondent put it, "he was working himself into an early grave".

Curtin's long-term health bears watching.

THE WAR LOAN.

Curtin also had been worried about the latest war loan. It had just closed, and had only **just** been fully subscribed, and only after it had been extended for a week. Given that previous loans had been over-subscribed, it indicated that the public was, for several obvious reasons, losing its fear and its enthusiasm for the war.

A psychologist summed up the situation.

Letters, Psychologist, Sydney. As a member of one of the Service teams which for the past seven weeks visited from four to six factories, offices, or business houses daily, I enumerate some of the many and varied reasons for their **refusal to subscribe to government war bonds**.

They were heavy taxation, lack of a guarantee that when the bonds were sold, at least the face value would be obtained, the necessity of dealing with stock brokers when negotiating bonds, term of the bonds too long, waste in public services, industrial unrest, and consequent loss of prestige by the Government, the abolition of overtime leaving wages on a pre-war level, while the cost of living has increased out of all proportion, and fear of the taxation authorities asking the source of moneys invested. These appeared the main reasons, and it was with difficulty that the objections were overcome.

Comment. He might have mentioned that the war crisis was over.

THE CAT IS AWAY

The **Acting** Prime Minister, Frank Forde, started making noises at the end of November about nationalising the airlines. You will remember that only a few months earlier a referendum had been defeated which asked the question of whether the population wanted industries to be socialised after the war. The answer came back as a pretty definite, "NO".

Nothing daunted, however, some Government Ministers, including Forde, began confidently issuing details of what the **new, nationalised airline** would look like. But now he was **not talking about after the war, but starting the process in the immediate future.** Some others of the perennially disruptive ministers, like Calwell, chimed in and talked about nationalising the banks, and other bastions of free enterprise, and this alarmed all those people who had voted "**NO**" in the referendum. **Had there in fact been such a referendum, or had it just been a dream?**

There were plenty of people who were vocal on the issue.

Letters, L Taylors. The Government's decision to take over all interstate airlines is one which removes any doubt of a plan to "muscle in" on the sweat and effort of private enterprise. On the occasion of the referendum, the people showed their solid aversion to increasing Government control, but Canberra air appears to shorten memories very effectively. If, however, the members of the Government still remember the people's answer to their "more power" proposals, this latest effort is simply another blatant disregard of the democratic principle of accepting the public desire. Splendid satisfaction given by the airline companies in the past has simply qualified them for the Government chopping-block.

Letters, A Hebblewhite. The advantages of a contractual relationship between the Government and an aircraft company are widely recognised in America and England, as full play is allowed for progress, efficiency, and improvements in design of aircraft. The Government concerns itself with the issue of a licence for the route, collects taxes from profit, and is free of liability if loss occurs.

The granting of a subsidy is a clear cut proposition when service is desired on unpayable routes.

We, in Australia, have every reason to dread the intrusion of union and job control into the conduct of our air services in the post-war period. The present Government must know full well that at all times they have had to accede, as in the case of the wharf-labourers, slaughtermen, coal-miners, to the demands by union bosses.

Letters, W Henson. The Government's recent decision to take over control of all interstate airways is a certain indication of its socialistic outlook. To date private companies have nursed Australian air transport through its infancy, and have overcome innumerable difficulties in the pioneering stage. Today they emerge as a creditable example of this country's ability to progress under the stimulus of private enterprise.

The elimination of healthy competition, coupled with the heavy drag of Government administration, may well spell the end of rapid progress in air transport in Australia. Too often have we witnessed the strangulation of private endeavour and the consequent nullification of the individual's ingenuity.

The recent referendum is indicative of the people's desire to prevent the dead hand of Government administration from interfering with private enterprise.

CLOTHING FOR MALES

The Government of this nation, being a bunch of jolly good fellows always anxious to please when cornered, accepted the bleeding obvious, and started to relieve some of the pressures that the citizenry were under. A few regulations here, and a few more there, were removed or reduced, and the regime became very slowly a bit more forgiving. Take for example the following strictures, on mens' clothing, that were released in December.

MEN'S AND BOYS' CLOTHING. Regulations will be changed to allow for the following in the clothing for men.

Coat-type shirts; extra buttons on men's and boys' shirt pocket in men's and boys' pyjamas; increased chest measurements on shirts to allow better fitting; welted or raised seams on all male outerwear; vents in overcoats of all types; full double-breasted lapels on jackets and coats of all types; trouser bottoms up to 22 inches; full double cuffs on trousers; extension bands on trouser waists (for self-supporting); half belts for boys' overcoats and boys' jackets; increased seams and hems.

DECEMBER NEWS ITEMS

The first of the hundreds of fishing trawlers, seized by the Navy almost three years ago, has been released, and has brought in a very good catch.

There is a **surplus of fully-trained crews in the RAAF**. The training of air-crew recruits will now be suspended.

With the approach of Christmas, **bottled beer** is bringing up to 70 shillings a dozen bottles **on the black market**. The official fixed price is 19 shillings per dozen.

By a majority of 2,800 votes, the population of the industrial NSW city of Newcastle voted (at a referendum) **to ban all organised sport on Sundays.** This was not just sport-for- profit, but all sport like cricket, and children's soccer and Rugby League. A high official of the United Church said that it was the first serious setback to **the forces attempting to paganise Sunday....**

The vote made little difference because of **the long-standing ban on Sunday sport at Council grounds by the local Council.** Most of the sport played was on Council grounds.

Japanese P-O-Ws being transferred round Queensland were occupying first class seats on the Brisbane Mail, while citizens were being left behind on the platforms.

The Federal Department of W.O.I. (don't ask me) had taken over the administration of Toys Orders at the beginning of the year. They operated with the co-operation of the Department of Education, the Kindergarten Union,

Sydney Day Nurseries, the Mothercraft Training School, Repatriation Commission, the Red Cross Society, the Army Repatriation Service, and the Salvation Army. This select group offered suggestions on what new toys were suitable for manufacture...

In early December, the Department said that **lambs' wool koalas, two feet high,** to be sold at five Pounds each, had been **banned from sale at Christmas this year**. Though, it added, the sale of small woolly dogs, at eight shillings, would be permitted....

A first criticism was the price was so high that few people would buy them. So it could **not be argued** by the wildest stretch of the imagination that **somehow the war effort was affected....**

Secondly, because there were **so many people involved in the decision-making**. Surely, it was suggested, this is the danger of control by Government. **Government had no right to be involved at all in what Christmas toys were offered for sale,** if the war effort was not threatened.

The Home Guard in Britain was made up of **four million men** who, for one reason or another, could not be used for military purposes, or for the equivalent of our CCC. Many of them were retired and some of them were in their seventies. On December 4th, a selected few of them **paraded for the King**, and **he officially allowed them to stand down. Dad's Army was on permanent leave.**

HIT SONGS, 1944

SWINGING ON A STAR	Bing Crosby
DON'T FENCE ME IN	Bing Crosby
I'll BE SEEING YOU	Vera Lynn
GOODNIGHT IRENE	Ella Fitzgerald
SATURDAY NIGHT IS LONELIEST	Frank Sinatra
ALWAYS HURT THE ONE YOU LOVE	Mills Brothers
THE TROLLEY SONG	Judy Garland
SHOO-SHOO-BABY	Andrew Sisters
MAIRZY DOATES	Merry Macs

TOP MOVIES

ARSENIC AND OLD LACE	Grant, Ray Massey
BUGS BUNNY ,THREE BEARS	Animated
DOUBLE INDEMNITY	McMurray, Stanwick
GOING MY WAY	Crosby, Fitzgerald
HOUSE OF FRANKENSTEIN	Boris Karloff
I'LL BE SEEING YOU	Rogers, Temple
KEYS OF THE KINGDOM	Gregory Peck, Mitchell
LOST IN A HAREM	Abbott and Costello
Mrs PARKINSON	Greer Garson, Pidgeon

THE WAR OVERSEAS

In Europe, almost everywhere, military victories were coming thick and fast, and in fact, too fast for me to give details. All over Europe, the Allies were having great victories.   Non-stop, every day. Occasionally the Axis forces would put up some   meaningful resistance, but the Allies had the reserves and materials to over-run the opposition.

On the western front, the Brits, Canadians and US were now just into Germany. On the eastern front, the Russians had won control of much of Poland and East Prussia in the north, and down to Bulgaria in the south. Greece was now mainly liberated, and the Germans had been pushed back to the mountains to the north of Italy.

At a terrible price, the Allied forces swept from one region to the next, taking an even more terrible toll on the enemy as they went. Germany was on the road to defeat, Hitler and his generals were divided, the German population was under constant threat from aerial bombs, food was sometimes scarce, and society in general was breaking down. It was clear now that, given winter always slowed armies down, there would be no Allied victory in Europe before Christmas, but it seemed likely in the first few months of next year.

A small point of dissonance in Europe. The newer German V2 rockets were still cruising the skies, with menace. These were faster and bigger than previous rockets, but they were more inclined to explode at the wrong time and place. Still, they were frightening for Londoners, and they would remain so until all their source sites could be located and destroyed.

Comment. This will be my final mention of the European war in this book. So I will point out that on December 16th, Hitler launched a major offensive into the region of the Ardennes, north of France. This is was well-known as the **Battle of the Bulge**. It had good successes early but, as always, the problems of an increasing supply-line became too much, and it petered out by mid-January.

Finally, in Europe, I will **steal the thunder from my next book** and remind you that the Germans continued to collapse, and ultimately surrendered unconditionally on May 8th, and Churchill called a public holiday to celebrate. Hitler committed suicide, most of his generals were captured and tried at Nuremberg in 1946, and thousands of his lesser military officers were hanged by local resistance groups.

The war in Europe was coming to an end. Amid the rejoicing let me remind you of two facts. Firstly, for many parts of Europe, the end of fighting did not bring the peace that was wanted. In country after country, various groups wanted power for themselves, and were prepared to fight to get that power. For example, Greece erupted into civil war, Poland had a running fight with the conquering Russians, various kings were gradually replaced in various nations. Hunger was rife. Life after the war was generally improved, but no nirvana.

Secondly, the fighting for years, and the victory, had come at a huge cost. **Britain lost comparatively** 260 thousand military, and 60,000 civilians. In Germany, the figures increased to 3 million men and 4 million civilians. Then, **the horrendous figures for Russia and the Balkans were 14 million military, and 6 million civilians.**

Comment. As you consider the enormity of these numbers, you might try to tell me just what form of madness and madmen created them. I say again, and I say it often, **no one wins a war.**

In Asia, again it was a parade of naval, land and air victories. Tokyo had just now come under **daily** air attack from Super Fortresses, the protective big ring of islands that dotted the Pacific were being invaded and won, the Jap fleet was in hiding, and losing ships at an alarming rate. In parts of China, the Japs were gaining some ground, but overall the Allies were trudging forward at a confidence-inspiring rate.

Comment. Again stealing my thunder from my 1945 year-book, I remind you that the Japs surrendered unconditionally on August 15th. Thirty thousand Australian men had lost their lives, and many more had been crippled, and maimed and damaged for life in prison camps, some of them for over three years. After three and a half years, the carnage had stopped, and no matter what else came and went, this nation was enormously relieved that this terrible bit of history was behind us.

THE NATION'S BIRTH-RATE

Serious thinkers were now turning to what would happen after the war was over. A few noted that the population of Australia had not shown much change during the war, and worried about how we could increase it when the hostilities stopped. This was a topic that would cause much discussion over the next few years, but here are a few of the earliest thoughts.

Letters, Mother of Only One. Much has been said recently about women who don't want families and many specified reasons are given, but few people realise that thousands of women in Australia would be only too pleased to have babies tomorrow if the opportunity were granted them. Many servicemen with five years' service have only had one or two leaves with their wives and great is the disappointment of both husband and wife when no babies are forthcoming.

I am one of the luckier ones and have a new baby, much to the envy of many of my friends, some of them over 35 years of age like myself, and no immediate prospects as the AIF have been promised again long tasks away from this country. I have known of some women, fearing they will soon be too old to have a child, **to break the border laws to cross into another State and live like fugitives** under difficult conditions with the main hope of a future family.

We have one child and would like at least four, but see little chance of this eventuating with my husband's record of already five years' service stretching into six or seven.

Letters, Mackie.   As a healthy woman quite capable of producing a dozen children I feel I must voice my story.   Recently I had my second child after a break of eight years.   My husband and I were very thrilled, but my mother threw up her hands in horror – "More worry! I can't say I am pleased. You are a fool to tie yourself down," etc. My mother-in-law said, "What have you been up to?", and another relative told me I was a "goat."

Mine is not an isolated case as I know several others willing to shoulder the bundle bearing as well as having children, but what they can't face is the criticism. The eligible mother of today does not expect help from all and sundry, but she does like to know those nearest and dearest to her are glad about the new little Australian, too. Until the mothers-to-be of our country are not treated like naughty children, no National Health Council will ever overcome this problem.

Comment. The reference, in the first Letter, to breaking the border laws refers to the **current restriction on persons moving to a different State without getting permission to do so**. Such permissions were virtually impossible to get, and took forever. So she could not move legally to a place near her husband's current camp and so get on with the job.

SHORTAGE OF NURSES.

Letters, Senior Schoolgirl. The daily appeal for trainees in the nursing profession has prompted me, a senior schoolgirl approaching her 18th birthday, to state why recruits are difficult to find. It is generally agreed that **the scrubbing-brush**

and bucket still occupy much of the trainee's time, while many hospitals regard student nurses **as rebellious children** who must be disciplined.

The accommodation offered at many hospitals is a disgrace. Girls who have their own bedroom at home do not like living in a dormitory with four or five other trainees. The recreation rooms are quite inadequate. The rates of pay are insufficient for most young women, whose parents are forced to contribute to their keep.

The educational standard required is far too low. Twenty years ago the Intermediate was some guide to a woman's standard of education, but nothing less than the Leaving Certificate should be asked now. If the latter certificate was required, the period of training could be reduced to two years – as in the United States, where the profession has progressed with the times.

Letters, Six Pounds Per Week. The plain fact is that the nursing profession does not appeal to the girls of today from an economic viewpoint, and whether the test for admittance as a trainee be one examination or two examinations or no examination at all, the hospitals cannot compete with the buses, trams, offices, factories, etc. As for making the Leaving Certificate the entrance test – this step would surely close the hospitals. An enormous number of people cannot cope with the Intermediate, so how would the Leaving Certificate examination provide trainees? If any test be considered necessary, vocational guidance and selection would be the ideal. The scrubbing brush and bucket are not to be despised, but I would be surprised if they are part of a nurse's training.

Letters, A Smith. It is to be hoped "Senior Schoolgirl" is not contemplating becoming a hospital trainee. How many girls have their own bedroom? What does she want elaborate recreation rooms for? If parents have brought up their girls so that they cannot manage on what hospitals now pay, it is their own fault if they have to supplement the salary.

I trained at Sydney Hospital, starting with 6/4 a week, and no other concessions – was put into a bedroom with three other girls. I liked the company, for we studied together, chatted and discussed our mistakes, etc. We certainly were strictly trained, but I never had anything but justice and kindness shown to me – and there was not a prouder young woman in NSW when I was given my certificates and references in 1917. My training has been my most valued asset. I was two years on active service. I was the only passenger on an ocean liner who could help with an urgent appendix. I was able to nurse my husband and my parents. My opinion is there is no cause for complaint for trainees.

Letters, Eleven Senior Nurses, Sydney. As senior nurses at one of Sydney's leading hospitals, we should like to reply to the misinformed statements contained in "Senior Schoolgirl's" letter. Is she aware that the scrubbing brush and bucket so disdainfully mentioned as occupying much of the trainee's time, are unjustly condemned? They have been, are, and will be a method of thoroughly cleansing certain articles, hospital or otherwise.

As for discipline, it is only an exceptional girl who, at the age of 18 years, acts continuously as a rebellious schoolgirl, and in any case, discipline hurts nobody; particularly when dealing with a patient's life. In the matter of accommodation we suggest that "Senior Schoolgirl" acquaint herself with existing conditions before condemning them. Some hospitals have more amenities than others – we are fully satisfied with our own.

In reference to salary: nursing is a profession, and what other profession receives as high remuneration before registration? The educational standard actually required of a nurse is one combining intelligence, aptitude, and adaptability. Theoretical attainments are of value when studying for hospital examinations, but the sought-after nurse is one who, with training, can assume responsibility and be trusted to act with every-day common sense. Twenty years ago there was no higher standard of education required than now. Is "Senior Schoolgirl" criticising those women who today are in positions of responsibility and have proved themselves capable of raising the nursing profession to the high standard of efficiency it now enjoys? If, as she suggests, the Leaving Certificate were required and the training period then reduced to two years, we would find a woman holding a nurse's certificate who would be little more than the schoolgirl who entered the training school – technically improved, but a nurse – no. Training in both theory and the practical knowledge of the theory, extending over a period of three years at least, is most necessary to provide the foundations of a good nurse – modern nursing still retains its original aim: the care of the sick.

Comment. I think it is true to say that, throughout my long life, there has always been a shortage of nurses all the time. Despite what the second Letter-writer said above, conditions for nurses in 1944 were really tough, and the discipline imposed on them was severe. Matrons were as tough as old boots, and sisters often imposed senseless rules and petty controls simply because the young lasses needed discipline. This was not just in the wards, on the job. Their lives in their quarters was carefully monitored, and when I recall that the nurses were allowed out only at the matron's whim, and that they were always subject to an early curfew, you will realise how intense it all was.

These young girls were the classic example of those who were overworked and underpaid.

CHRISTMAS GIFTS

If you are looking for Christmas presents in this 1944 year, and if you are on a tight budget, I can suggest:

The Search for the Golden Boomerang, for a 10-year-old boy.

Barefoot in the Forest, for a 13-year-old boy

Emily of new Moon, for a 16-year-old girl

When given with lots of obvious love, they will do the trick.

SUMMING UP 1944

By the end of the year, it was obvious that the Battle of the Bulge was not going to stop the Allies' advances, and that Hitler had played his last trump card. Even for the biggest pessimist, it was clear that the two wars would grind to an end sometime next year.

So, for all Australians the prospects for next year were better than they had been at this time last year. In fact, the thought of an imminent peace raised the spirit of everyone. Granted, those who had lost men continued to grieve, and those who had men in prison camps, and those who had no idea where their menfolk were, all of these had their own crosses to bear. But, even for these, the end of the slaughter would be God-send.

The more optimistic of citizens, and these were the majority, had an idea that we might soon approach Nirvana. There was a notion that this indeed had been **the war to end all wars**, and that peace and harmony would descend upon earth. It turned out that they were wrong. Within a year, the world was dividing again into goodies and baddies, into Capitalists and Communists, along either side figuratively of a soon-to-be Iron Curtin. Within this nation, the Labour Party still persisted with its pursuit of socialism, and the Uniting Party (soon to be the Liberals) maintained its policy of helping business, especially big business. In brief, **on all fronts**, confrontation and division were the order of the day. This was not at all peaceful, but **perhaps it was as close to it as mankind will ever get.**

Be that as it may, the nation's citizens looked forward to a much happier year. They knew that austerity was still with them, but assumed (wrongly) that it would soon go away. They thought (wrongly) that the housing crisis would soon be fixed. They believed (wrongly) that their menfolk would come home and be slotted back into the workforce without problems. They had ideas about lots of things, and even if they were not wrong on all of these, most of them turned out differently from what was expected.

They also believed (correctly) that when the Servicemen returned, everyone's entire world would be different. Women and men by the million had seen that **the restrictive static pre-war world of hopelessness and drudgery did not have to be their lot in the future.** All of them had seen new worlds, felt the freedom generated by mobility and adventure, and wanted none of it for the future. The fact that a million women and a million men quickly tied themselves down to a family does not gainsay any of this, because they now had the wonderful feeling generated by the security of freedom and independence, and **they passed it on by the bucket-load to their Baby-Boom children.**

If it turns out that if you were one of these children, think for a moment about how lucky you were and are, and **wonder what life would have been like if there had been no war.**

In 1950, Dugan and Mears used a hacksaw to break out of gaol, robbed banks, shot people and went back to gaol. The War finished five years ago, so it was time to stop petrol rationing. War criminals were hanging out at Nuremberg. Dancing pumps were tripping the light fantastic at The Plaza. Whaling in Australia was big; square dancing was bigger.

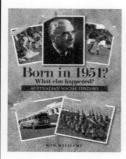

In 1951, the coal miners' funds were declared black. The great mower war disturbed Sunday's peace. General MacArthur was given the boot. Hire purchase was buying vacuum cleaners. Sunday films and sport were driving clergy frantic. Farmers were hopping mad over a kangaroo glut.

****

Chrissi and birthday books for Mum and Dad, Grandma and Pop, and Aunt and Uncle and cousins and family and friends and work and everyone else.

Don't forget a good read and chuckle for yourself.

In 1952, Bob (Menzies) was not your uncle. Women smokers were keeping the home fires burning. Sid Barnes jumped a turnstile and suited himself. US and China were still happily killing each other, and millions of Koreans were collateral damage. Some horses were entering a grey area. Women voted to do jury duty at their convenience.

****